Praise for *Choosing Easy World*

"Julia's simple, clear way of explaining the universal truth about the flow of abundance in our world will be an eye-opener for many who've wondered if there were an easier path in life. Her message is an anchor of safety whenever we become adrift in fear and the seeming hardship of life. We truly do live in Easy World, as Julia has had the incredible perception to see."

—Summer McStravick, author of *Flowdreaming*

"Allow Julia Rogers Hamrick to show you the way to a free-flowing world filled with abundance, joy, well-being, and love, and you will be amazed at how easy it really is! Whatever you are doing right now, put it aside and immerse yourself in the brilliance of your new Easy World."

—Peggy McColl, *New York Times* bestselling author of *Your Destiny Switch*

"*Choosing Easy World* reminds us to create the world we wish to live in by letting go of control and opening up to the Divine Good, which is ever-present around us. Julia Rogers Hamrick's joy for life jumps off the pages and lands soundly in your heart."

—Kala Ambrose, host of the *Explore Your Spirit with Kala Show* and author of *9 Life Altering Lessons: Secrets of the Mystery Schools Unveiled*

"*Choosing Easy World* is an amazing book designed for anyone wishing to learn the true wisdom of life: It will teach you how to emerge from challenges and discover the Easy World we were all granted but sometimes neglect. It helps one unlock the potential for a resilient life and rejoice in everyday miracles."

—Dr. Carmen Harra, author of *The Eleven Eternal Principles*

"*Choosing Easy World* is a must-read! In it, Julia Rogers Hamrick provides a refreshing perspective on how each and every one of us can create an Easy World to live in no matter what. I love this book!"

—Eva Gregory, author of *The Feel Good Guide to Prosperity* and co-author of *Life Lessons for Mastering the Law of Attraction*

"Absolutely awesome! Julia's writing gripped me from the first sentence. *Choosing Easy World* is a masterpiece with highly original concepts, answers, and solutions. I recommend this gem to everyone. You will be thankful you read it—it will change your life."

—Barbara Rose, Ph.D., bestselling author of
If God Hears Me, I Want an Answer!

"A must-read for anyone who's ready to give up doing life the hard way and start living in Easy World! Julia Rogers Hamrick gives us the keys to unlock the door so we may step into this world effortlessly. *Choosing Easy World* is full of inspiration, spiritual wisdom, and practical tools guiding you toward a greater awakening for a life filled with peace, joy, and ease!"

—Linda Salazar, author of *Awaken the Genie Within*

"There's a little magic hidden in the pages of this book. Once a reader begins it, no matter how cynical they may be, the words 'I choose Easy World' keep slipping into their consciousness. Immediately, miracles start happening. I read this book on a busy day when I had an overwhelming list of things to do. By the end of the day, I was a firm believer in the magic of Easy World and of Julia Hamrick's user-friendly formula for accessing it."

—Sue Frederick, author of *I See Your Dream Job:
A Career Intuitive Shows You How to Discover
What You Were Put on Earth to Do*

"For those who feel you must fight to attain, Julia Rogers Hamrick's paradigm-shifting new book, *Choosing Easy World,* brings a radical simplicity, grace, and joy to everyday 'reality.' It is the option to exist in the world of your choosing, offering the choice to live in grace. Take a deep breath, open your heart, and decide to live the life of ease . . . by choosing Easy World."

—Nancy Lee, spiritual intuitive psychotherapist, author, radio host, and
president of SPRE, the Society for PSI Research and Education

"This masterpiece really is the quintessential guide to a life of one's dreams. This isn't just another Law of Attraction book that is rehashing the same thing. Other L.O.A. books talk about raising one's vibration but don't give easily applicable steps saying how to do it. *Choosing Easy World* provides step-by-step, easy-to-understand concepts and easy-to-apply action steps to truly find a life of joy, love, prosperity, and dare I say bliss. Who doesn't want an Easy World life? Outstanding!"

—Suze Baez, international speaker, coach, and philosopher

"I love *Choosing Easy World*! This is a remarkable book—easy to understand, simple, uplifting, and entertaining to read. Life is indeed simple, easy, fun, and productive in Easy World. It's the only smart way to live! Thank you, Julia, for gifting us with the golden key to the door into Easy World. I choose to live in Easy World!"

—Venus Andrecht, author and radio host, www.GodIsAlwaysHappy.com

"This little gem of a book will move you right out of Difficult World and into the wonderful realm of Easy World, where we all belong. Breathe, relax, and enjoy your way to the place where everything works out easily and effortlessly. There's no place like Easy World!"

—Chellie Campbell, author of *The Wealthy Spirit* and *Zero to Zillionaire*

Choosing

Easy World™

*A Guide to Opting Out of Struggle and Strife and Living
in the Amazing Realm Where Everything Is Easy*

JULIA ROGERS HAMRICK

ST. MARTIN'S PRESS ✖ NEW YORK

www.stmartins.com

Book design by Ruth Lee-Mui

Library of Congress Cataloging-in-Publication Data

Hamrick, Julia Rogers.
    Choosing easy world : a guide to opting out of struggle and strife and living in the amazing realm where everything is easy / Julia Rogers Hamrick. — 1st ed.
        p. cm.
    ISBN 978-0-312-62363-0
    1. New Age movement.   I. Title.
    BP605.N48H353 2010
    299'.93—dc22

                                                          2009045737

First Edition: August 2010

10   9   8   7   6   5   4   3   2   1

Dedicated to

YOU

*and the multitudes of other Easy World expatriates
ready to return home*

Contents

Introduction

The World of Your Origins

I'm going to tell you a story about you. If you don't immediately remember it, just know that a kind of amnesia is
responsible for that. It may seem like a fantasy, and if it feels
best to you to think of it that way, please allow yourself to just
relax and go there in your imagination.

Whatever way you think of it, I believe a familiarity will begin to emerge as you read, stirring your primal memories and
awakening the longing within you to embrace the world and
the ways of your origins once more.

The world with which you are probably most familiar is not
your original world. Your origins are in a far kinder, gentler
place—a place of ease, fulfillment, and joy. You thrived there.
Your current tumultuous reality may be fascinating, but it is
not your true home. Your present reality, which has been so

Breathe...Relax...Allow...Enjoy

acute in your consciousness and has moved you to such a different experience of life from the one you started out with, has all but blocked out your awareness of how things were—and how they can be again.

Yes, the reality state in which you dwell at present provides a magnificent experience of extreme contrast: sadness, which creates a longing for joy; pain and violence, which create a longing for peace; difficulty, which creates a longing for ease. But when do these longings get fulfilled? When you learn to choose Easy World.

What we are longing for is Home. That's where our cravings for joy, peace, and ease are fulfilled. And we can absolutely choose to be there. I will show you how.

First, let me refresh your memory.

Once upon a time, everything was easy. Whatever you needed, you had. No sweat. You didn't struggle. You didn't strive. You didn't worry. You just enjoyed life, allowed whatever you needed or desired to be provided for you, did what interested and energized you, and experienced joy and fulfillment. You lived in Easy World.

In Easy World, you lacked nothing; you were immersed in a free-flowing stream of well-being and Love, and anything you needed simply came to you in that flow. It never occurred to you that something you needed or desired would be difficult to come by because it never was. You always allowed and never resisted this flow of abundant supply. Nor did you have any-

Breathe...Relax...Allow...Enjoy

thing superfluous—you always had the right amount of every-thing.

In Easy World, all that you did was inspired. If you felt joyful energy rising up in you to do something, you took action, and the task was fun and easy. If a possible action was presented to you and you didn't feel the energy naturally increasing in re-sponse, you simply didn't act, because the action was not yours to take.

You never did anything because of external motivation in Easy World. No "shoulds" or "oughts" or "supposed-tos" were part of your life. No one in Easy World would ever suggest to you that something you were not internally motivated to do was yours to do. That mind-set is utterly foreign in the world of your origins! Similarly, you never resisted doing something that *was* yours to do, or failed to respond to inspiration. That, too, was inconceivable.

You waited to be inspired and motivated from within, with the energy welling up in you to match whatever it was you were inspired to do. You were impelled at exactly the right time to do precisely that which would enhance and prosper the Whole of Creation—including yourself, of course.

In Easy World, everything is in harmony with everything else because everyone is attuned with its innate design: the De-sign for Harmony. And everything that needs to be done is done in perfect sequence and order. You might call it "timing," but it is a timing that has nothing to do with clocks. You never need a clock because the attunement of all to the heartbeat of

Breathe...Relax...Allow...Enjoy

Easy World is what governs the order and rate at which things unfold in perfect coordination there.

In your original state, you were fulfilled but never, ever bored. You poured yourself into doing what you felt the most excited about and eager to do. You accomplished things with the greatest of ease because everything you did suited your nature and was in alignment with your passions. Any challenge you experienced was not because of conflict; it was because you chose it for fun.

You were continually open to ever-increasing new levels of fascination, and you entertained and delighted yourself by expressing your innate creativity without limits. You had total support from universal forces, which always supplied you with everything you needed for your creations simply by your thinking of it and then allowing it to show up in your reality. You never blocked the appearance of anything you desired by doubt; in Easy World, you always had total confidence that it would appear in perfect order, because it always did.

Conflict and turmoil were not a part of your experience in Easy World, because they don't exist there. The currents of Love energy are so powerful in Easy World that opposing forces can't exist, and thus are not able to create friction in that realm. Peace is the underlying state in Easy World, and harmony is a given. Anything other than peace and harmony is simply unheard-of.

There was never a need for healing in the home of your origins, because there was no such thing as wounding or disease.

Breathe...Relax...Allow...Enjoy

Dis-ease, or a lack of *ease,* just can't exist in Easy World! (Return-ing to Easy World when you've been away from it, however, is healing because its powerful, magnetic state of wholeness brings you into alignment with the innate wholeness that underlies your very design.)

In this reality, joy was your predominant emotion. Quiet contentment was at the low end of your emotional spectrum in Easy World, and total bliss, at the high end. You were all kinds of happy in your original home, following your Spirit, trusting in and aligning with the Design for Harmony, maintaining your vibration at the highest levels, and loving life and the infi-nite pleasures to be partaken of. Your capacity for joy was un-bounded.

Yes, this was your world—your easy, blissful world—the only reality you knew.

One day, however, you asked for a new kind of adventure, one that would broaden your experience. And so, you made a choice that delivered you to a different world, one that was foreign to you in every way.

In this world, things are hard, and conflict and pain are commonplace. Fighting for what you want and against what you don't want is considered normal. Struggle is celebrated in this world—in this difficult world. In Difficult World, instead of trusting things to get done in the flow, human beings believe they must swim upstream and *make* things happen.

They believe they must work hard and sacrifice to have what they need—if they believe they can get it at all. They believe

Breathe...Relax...Allow...Enjoy

that there is never enough to go around, and that they must fight for their share. They believe that there are forces working against them, and that other people are out to get them. They believe they must defer their joy and freedom until they achieve certain goals. They believe they must do things that don't fit their true nature or support their joy in order to survive.

This is what people are taught in Difficult World, and this is the code by which they live their lives. You were taught these things, too. And before you knew it, you were caught up in them, living your life more and more in alignment with these life-depleting ways than with the life-enhancing ways of your origins.

Thus, from your harmonious world of bounteous, free-flowing blessings and "Easy does it," you found yourself in the midst of "never enough," "No pain, no gain," and "If you don't have to work hard for it, it's not worth having." Even though the memories of Easy World were still deep inside, they started to fade as you began to buy into these strange notions.

As you can see, you were—and are—totally out of your element in Difficult World: the proverbial fish out of water. But with the help of the other residents of this foreign reality, over time you became more and more acclimated to it, and came to believe that you had to adopt the tenets and ways of Difficult World in order to survive, when nothing could be farther from the truth.

Though once enfolded in a realm of joy and fulfillment, you now found yourself immersed in a realm of struggle and frus-

Breathe...Relax...Allow...Enjoy

tration, with only fleeting glimpses of joy. Soon, you forgot about Easy World altogether, and forgot you had *chosen* to leave it, and thus, that you could choose to return.

Marooned as you now were in Difficult World, your life became about solving problems and surviving stress. Instead of living with ease from the deep knowing that you are totally supported by the Design for Harmony the way you once did, you have felt unsupported, finding yourself aligned with the Design for Disharmony, and *experiencing* disharmony and dis-ease as a result.

You certainly got the new experience you had asked for! But now that you have had lots of experience living a Difficult World life, you may be ready to release yourself from the trap you created for yourself. You may be ready to live an easier life again. If so, I have fabulous news!

It's time to rediscover Easy World, the reality of your origins—the state of being in which you don't simply survive, you *thrive*. It's time to come home to the reality in which you are fully supported in being your Self and doing what is in alignment with your heart's desires. It's time to come home to the reality where things work out without your having to break a sweat—unless you want to.

It's time to relearn to allow the flow of universal forces to bring you all that you need and desire without struggle. It's time to experience harmony as your foundation and to feel supported by the Design for Harmony once again. It's time to experience the true empowerment that only being in Easy World

Breathe...Relax...Allow...Enjoy

can provide. It's time to remember that being in Easy World is a decision you can make at any time, and that if you decide to revisit Difficult World, you recognize that it's a *choice,* not a necessity.

It's time to reclaim your birthright of ease and joy once more. Even though you may have departed Easy World, it still exists as it has from the time of first creation, and it is always ready to welcome you home.

Easy World is calling. Come on! I'll show you the way!

I choose to live in Easy World,

where everything is easy.

1

Rediscovering Easy World

ake up! Wake up! I have exciting news! It's time to return to Easy World at last!

Long ago, you fell asleep and found yourself in Difficult World and forgot you had the choice to be in the world in which your life is easy and joy-filled. You've been spending the majority of your life in the realm of struggle, strife, and worry, not realizing it was unnecessary. But now it's time to rediscover the remarkable world of your origins and to remember that you can choose to be there once more.

Even though you—and the rest of humanity—have pretty much forgotten about it, the reality called "Easy World" is eternal. It exists as it has since before the dawn of human existence and is as vital and powerful as ever. It has been perpetually available and accessible to every single human being at any

Breathe...Relax...Allow...Enjoy

time (and yes, that includes you), but because you forgot about it and didn't know to choose it, it may as well not have existed except for those times when you slipped back into it unawares.

Basically, *it* never went away—*you* did!

But however long you've been away, Easy World is waiting for you to remember it. And because the more of us who choose Easy World, the more harmonious and joyful life on Planet Earth will be, I believe we're getting extra help now in remembering. As you will see when you read my personal story of rediscovering Easy World, which I'm going to share with you in this chapter, Easy World is *so* ready for our return, it apparently has invisible PR agents, intent on helping us remember it!

I certainly needed help. I'd like to assure you from the outset that my being the one to bring you the word about Easy World is *not* because I am the extremely rare human being who has managed to stay in Easy World her whole life, never losing touch with it. Not at all. I think I was simply ripe to return to it, and Divine Intelligence knew I was someone who would never keep quiet about such an amazing discovery!

Just as I'm sure you have, I have spent a large share of my life outside of Easy World. In all honesty, I still find myself in Difficult World more than I'd like to, though *far* less often than before I was reawakened to an awareness of Easy World and my choice to be there! In fact, it was my unconscious insistence on being in Difficult World at a particular time that seemed to beckon the remembrance of Easy World.

I'm going to share my own story of rediscovering Easy World

Breathe...Relax...Allow...Enjoy

with you now so you can see how quickly and easily one can move out of Difficult World and into Easy World again, even after a long, long absence—and even when there is every reason to believe that things are so complicated, they surely *have* to be difficult!

A DIVINE WHISPER

I was reminded of Easy World, appropriately, at the easiest possible time for me to be receptive to it: when I was way, *way* outside of it. It was about 4:20 in the morning—you know, that time when you wake up and start thinking about the pile of things facing you but it's too early (sane people are still sleeping) to take practical steps to deal with whatever you're worried about, so you just lie there stewing. I bet you've been there before.

My husband, Rick, and I had just the evening before clinched our decision to install an Endless Pool, a small swimming pool with a current you swim against, in our garage. We had met with the installer, figured out the logistics, and set a time line. While this was cause for celebration—a dream coming true after my having wanted the pool for almost twenty years, and now *needing* one because of knee problems—it was going to require a whole lot more than just setting up a small pool in the garage!

I won't name all the items on the mile-long list of tasks that needed orchestrating, and stuff that had to be moved, excavated, cleaned, built, installed, and paid for. It was a mammoth-seeming undertaking, requiring multiple tradespeople, including concrete contractors, building contractors, electrical contractors, and so on. And all of this had to be perfectly coordinated to get everything done by the time the pool arrived to be installed, with a substantial financial penalty for not being ready. No pressure there!

There was a whole pile of additional factors, too, including harsh winter weather (this was Denver, Colorado, at the end of January 2007, with frozen ground covered by feet-deep, frozen-solid snow) and the timing of other home improvement projects that had already been scheduled. Oh, and I can't fail to mention that the garage was housing a couple dozen cartons of books, our larger-than-average collection of lawn and garden equipment and supplies, and years' worth of miscellaneous junk that we had stuck there when we didn't know what else to do with it.

Talk about overwhelming—where was all this stuff going to go? With my mobility issues and Rick's work commitments, how were we going to get it all cleaned out and moved so the contractors could get started? And speaking of contractors, how would we find the right ones?

My past experience with contractors had been that not many were interested in small jobs, so I deeply dreaded trying to get anyone to say he'd be willing to do the work, not to mention interviewing a bunch of contractors to try to find the best price for the best quality, and orchestrate it all so it got done in the right sequence and on time. Consider my anxiety about coordinating all this, combined with my perfectionistic need to get it all exactly right, and you'll have some sense of my state of mind upon retiring that night.

I went to bed in a knot of concern, but not before I filled out a few requests with an Internet company I had received a promotional e-mail about earlier that week that matches you with prescreened contractors in your area. I didn't have much confidence in it, but at least it was a way to feel I was doing something, even though it was late at night. I planned to start the uncomfortable task of getting out the phone book and making cold calls the next day.

As is my habit as a night owl, I went to bed at around two A.M., and when I woke up at 4:20, all of this was on my mind. As I lay there, mind churning, desperately trying to figure out how in the world I was going to make this all happen the way it needed to, I heard a gentle, loving, yet firm inner whisper that said what I now know were some of the most profound words I'd ever heard: "Julia, you *could* just choose to live in Easy World, where everything is easy."

Easy World? It sounded like a refreshing oasis in the midst of a vast desert, and something deep inside said, *"Yes!"*

Too mentally exhausted from all the worry and lack of sleep to question or ponder what I'd heard, I realized I might as well let go, since I seemed to be getting nowhere anyway. "What the heck?" I thought. There seemed to be nothing to lose.

And then I said, "Okay. I choose to live in Easy World, where everything is easy." I rolled over, relaxed, promptly fell asleep, and slumbered in complete peace.

Breathe...Relax...Allow...Enjoy

Awakening to a Whole New World

By the time I woke up mid-morning and got to my desk, I had forgotten about Easy World. Remarkably, however, I had e-mails and calls from multiple contractors for each job that needed doing. While I had forgotten about Easy World, it, apparently, had not forgotten about me! Things fell into place with an ease that was simply unprecedented in my experience, and it was obvious something very different was going on.

I didn't have to beat the bushes for people willing to do the work; I had an abundance of people lined up to do it! We met with the first contractor who had contacted us about doing the concrete work, and not only did we feel very comfortable with him, but he and his crew were also itching to start immediately. And, though he had answered our request for concrete work, he was a general contractor.

Except for the electrical work, his crew could do everything we needed to have done, including all the carpentry. Perhaps most amazing of all, they were *so* eager to start that in order to expedite things, the contractor volunteered his guys to clear all the stuff out of our garage—no small feat with books that needed to be relocated to the basement—at *no charge* just so they could go ahead and get to work! On their first day, they accomplished the emptying of the garage in thirty minutes flat and hardly broke a sweat.

Easy World? I was catching on!

While I was on the phone that day with my webmaster, Easy

World magic struck again. I had asked him to add something to my Web site—something a little out of the ordinary. He wasn't sure how to do it, and I could tell he was anticipating that it would be difficult, so I told him about Easy World and invited him in.

When I finished talking, I was met with dead silence. I thought he either had not been listening or had blown off what I had said. But after a few seconds, he said, somewhat incredulously, "What do you know? I found the script to do it and it's done! How easy was that?!" He had accepted my invitation into Easy World. I was thrilled. I loved discovering that it wasn't something that only I was able to tune in to.

That afternoon at rush hour, I went to my favorite natural-foods grocery store, located on a high-traffic main thoroughfare. There is a "No left turn" sign as you exit the parking lot, and left is the direction I need to go to get home from there. My usual course is to turn right out of the parking lot, take the first right after that, which leads up a steep hill, then make the next right, which takes me on a neighborhood street to the main road I turn right on to get home—a little out of the way, but normally not much of a problem.

We'd had a particularly harsh winter in Denver, however, and many neighborhood roads had not been plowed after multiple snows, making them rutted and icy. We'd had snow just the night before, too, so I knew my normal route up and around the block would be treacherous. I found myself beginning to worry and immediately caught myself. I said, "I choose to live in

Breathe...Relax...Allow...Enjoy

Easy World, where everything is easy. Getting home will be a piece of cake!"

Once I was inside the store, the shopping was pleasant and easy. At checkout time, the total of my purchases was $88.88. I love master numbers, and took this as a little wink from Spirit. As I left the store, I was prepared to find an alternate route home through the traffic and icy roads. But as I was exiting the parking lot, I looked both ways and *there was not a single car in sight*! At 5:30 P.M. on a usually clogged seven-lane road in a major metropolitan area at rush hour, there was no traffic at all.

This was completely unprecedented in my experience, and definitely *otherworldly*. Clearly, I was in another world, indeed! So I did what I figured anyone being presented with such a gift would do and, though it was discouraged (but not illegal) in Difficult World, I made what was clearly an Easy World–sanctioned left turn, and made it home in record time with no problems whatsoever.

I was beginning to feel right at home in Easy World.

A Universal Solution to All Problems

As I remembered to invoke Easy World over the ensuing days and weeks, I began to see that choosing Easy World worked for everything, and that the ideal was to live life entirely in Easy World. But the habit of Difficult World was ingrained, and so I needed to keep choosing Easy World whenever I recognized that I had fallen out of it, which was frequently.

Breathe...Relax...Allow...Enjoy

However frustrating it was each time to realize I was back in Difficult World, I was grateful that I now at least knew I had a choice! As I exercised that choice more and more, my overall experience of life began to be more harmonious, more joyful, and . . . easier!

Things that had felt stuck before seemed to be on the move again. My creativity was greatly increasing, and when I remembered to invoke Easy World, I found myself reveling in my writing, teaching, and other creative projects instead of struggling with them, and I saw that they were making a greater difference in the lives of others. It seemed that a lot of energy was freed up by my relaxing more and worrying less. And worrying was definitely a habit.

Not long after I first rediscovered Easy World and experienced its magic to arrange things to support ease and joy and alleviate worry, the two youngest of my beloved stepdaughters were in our charge. The younger of the two, Claire, who did not yet drive, had gone to an activity at the high school, and the next-to-youngest, Wendy, who'd had her license for just under a year, was hanging out at our house.

Claire was supposed to call when she needed to be picked up, and since Wendy would already be going out around that time to go home to their mom's house, where they lived, she had agreed to pick up Claire and drive them both home when the time came so that Rick wouldn't have to make a special trip out.

The roads were still icy, and I was a little concerned about her driving on them beyond the short distance home, but this is a girl

Breathe . . . Relax . . . Allow . . . Enjoy

who had grown up in Colorado and had taken a driving course that provided instruction and experience in extreme driving conditions, so I tried to reassure myself with that and relax about it. I'd like to say I was cool with the situation, but that would be an exaggeration.

Then, Claire didn't call when I thought she'd be calling, and I became more concerned. Adding to that, seeing that Wendy was napping as she waited, I worried even more about sending the groggy teen off into the night on dicey roads to fetch her sister.

Just as I was about to insist that Rick go to the high school to check on Claire and pick her up, I caught myself spinning problems out of thin air and remembered Easy World. I told myself to chill out. "I choose to live in Easy World, where everything is easy," I said to myself, and, feeling better immediately, I settled in for the EW solution to present itself.

Within a few minutes, the phone rang and it was Claire. "Please tell Dad he doesn't need to come get me. Mom is here and she's taking me home."

Easy World.

It's Your Turn to Choose Easy World!

From orchestrating major projects and sorting out impossible-seeming problems to dealing with the most ordinary, everyday stuff such as safety issues, general worries, and simple matters of

Breathe...Relax...Allow...Enjoy

convenience, it was made clear to me that choosing to be in Easy World was absolutely the way to go. And it gets clearer every day.

As this book unfolds, you'll read about many more of my experiences in Easy World, and about those of other people who have rediscovered Easy World as well. I expect you will soon have EW stories of your own, too! Consider me one of Easy World's PR agents, who has been tapped to make sure you do.

Life is just amazing when you spend it in Easy World, and I am eager for you to rediscover and experience it. As you move forward with your remembrance of Easy World, know that it stands ready for your return so that you can experience life the way it was originally intended for you to live it—with ease and joy.

Now that you know it's waiting for you, would you like the key to Easy World? You're in luck. I'll tell you where to find it in the next chapter!

I choose to live in Easy World,

where everything is easy.

Breathe...Relax...Allow...Enjoy

2

The Key to Easy World

As you may have picked up from reading about my own first forays back to Easy World, returning there is an extremely simple process. That may come as a relief after assuming, as so many of us have, that there must be some kind of special, complicated technique to learn if you want to unlock the door to bliss! You don't have to light candles, burn incense, quiet your mind, go to a special place, or even be centered—though those things certainly won't hurt.

Not only is accessing Easy World a simple process, you absolutely do not have to be in some sort of rarefied or lofty state in order to do it. Wherever you are in consciousness, Easy World is just a choice, a few key words, and a breath away.

Stressed to the max? Easy World is waiting. In a pickle? The door to Easy World is open. Disheartened? Confused? Ex-

Breathe...Relax...Allow...Enjoy

hausted? Just plain tired of Difficult World? The welcome mat is out. You can get to Easy World immediately from wherever you are whenever you realize you need to be there.

Now, for the key.

THE MAGIC WORDS THAT OPEN THE DOOR TO EASY WORLD

Once you become aware that you want to move into Easy World, you reinforce your choice by making a specific statement. Just like Ali Baba opened the cave of treasures using the words "Open, sesame," when you're ready to enter Easy World, you say the "magic" words that are what I call the Easy World invocation.

The Easy World invocation is the sentence I said when I was cued by the divine whisper I told you about in the previous chapter, and it goes like this: *I choose to live in Easy World, where everything is easy.*

Just say that, either aloud or silently, and that's it. The door is open!

GOING THROUGH THE DOOR

Now, to go through that door and enter Easy World, there are a few very simple but extremely important actions to take. You just *breathe, relax, allow,* and *enjoy.* Very, very easy.

That's really all you need to know, but just for fun, let's examine the various elements of the process so that we can understand

Breathe...Relax...Allow...Enjoy

the significance and purpose behind each part, starting with the Easy World invocation: "I choose to live in Easy World, where everything is easy."

"I CHOOSE"

While at first glance, these words may not look all that significant, they are a very important part of the Easy World invocation, especially when you are new to Easy World. Your saying "I choose" means that your conscious mind is aware it is making a choice and is testifying to this. It is signifying its agreement to leave Difficult World, and its decision to let go of trying to "drive" so that you can approach life the Easy World way. (We'll talk more about your mind and its relationship with Easy World farther along in the book.)

After you become practiced at moving into Easy World, you may be able to get by with dropping "I choose" and simply saying "I live in Easy World, where everything is easy." Sometimes, that will really feel like the right thing to say. Personally, I say it that way when I'm feeling sassy! But for now, keep "I choose" in place. In the beginning, at least, it is vital that the whole of you is aware that you are making a voluntary decision to move into Easy World.

"TO LIVE"

These words, too, seem pretty obvious. You may wonder if you can substitute another verb phrase like "to drive," such as in

"I choose *to drive* in Easy World, where everything is easy." Or "I choose *to heal* in Easy World, where everything is easy." Or "I choose *to make dinner* in Easy World, where everything is easy."

Well . . . yes. Absolutely. But in the beginning, I advise you to use the words "to live," because that signifies that you're choosing to move fully and completely into Easy World. It covers all the bases, including driving, healing, making dinner—everything. And when you fully understand what Easy World is, you will realize that you do truly *live* there, as opposed to in Difficult World, where life is continually undermined.

Besides, I have come to recognize through personal experience that the words with which I was provided in the magical moment when I was first given notice of Easy World were not random; they are the most powerful.

What you might want to try saying if you prefer something more specific to the activity at hand is: "I choose to live in Easy World, where everything is easy, including driving" (or healing or making dinner or whatever fits the situation). I have found that to work especially well for me.

"IN EASY WORLD"

When you say the name of Easy World, it confirms that there is an actual domain you're moving into, that you're going to be operating in the realm of ease. It sets you up for a shift in your sense of place. And Easy World truly is another place. As we'll

Breathe . . . Relax . . . Allow . . . Enjoy

discuss more thoroughly in the next chapter, it is a parallel reality—a reality that exists simultaneously with and adjacent to Difficult World, at a higher vibrational frequency.

As for the word "in," as in "in Easy World," you are telling yourself you are about to be ensconced in this different reality. You are going to be embraced and enfolded by it. How wonderful that feels!

"WHERE EVERYTHING IS EASY"

"Where everything is easy" describes the very nature of Easy World. This phrase is the icing on the cake for your logic-loving mind because it provides the *reason* for choosing Easy World, and the conscious mind always seems to need an incentive to do anything, especially when it comes to changing the status quo.

You might call this phrase "the hook" to ensure that EW is an appealing-sounding place. Of course, you are usually pretty motivated already when you're choosing Easy World, because if you need to choose it, it means you're in Difficult World!

READY, SET, GO!

Now put it all together and say the magic words: *"I choose to live in Easy World, where everything is easy."*

Once you do, you are there!

Welcome to Easy World! Come on in!

Breathe...Relax...Allow...Enjoy

THE EASY WORLD ACTIONS

In order to move into Easy World, to really *be* there and experience the Easy World magic, there are some things to do—very natural, easy things—that will assist you in bringing your whole self fully into EW and in ensuring that you don't find yourself right back in Difficult World.

BREATHE . . .

As soon as you say the invocation, take a deep breath in, allow it to circulate throughout your body, and then let it go, and with it, all of the tension and hyper energy you picked up in Difficult World. Just let it flow right on out. As you continue to breathe, imagine that you are breathing in the delicious air of Easy World, and let it fill you up with its energy.

RELAX . . .

You will now be at a point of relaxation. Consciously let go of any remaining physical and mental stress, and any resistance you may be holding on to. Release your concerns—just withdraw energy from them. Pretend you're letting all the "starch" out of your muscles and become as pliant as is easily possible.

Let your mind go blank for a second—as if you're changing gears in a car and you're putting the car in neutral—so that you become available to be pulled into alignment by the powerful magnetic force of the Design for Harmony. Feel it attracting you easily into it. (More about that in the next chapter.)

Breathe...Relax...Allow...Enjoy

ALLOW . . .

Allowing is the real linchpin for Easy World. It is the single most important aspect of your EW experience, since without allowing, you are not in Easy World, but back in Difficult World. Allowing means that you have not only dropped resistance to the mighty draw of Easy World's force field, but also that you are no longer mentally attempting to interfere with the operation of universal forces in alignment with the Design for Harmony.

It means you are no longer trying to figure things out or make them happen or otherwise control things. It means you are letting intelligent universal forces, operating together in harmony on behalf of your total well-being, do their magic to work things out without your trying to *make* them work out.

This, of course, requires faith that if you stop interfering, things will work out even better, and certainly faster, than if you are continually attempting to control them. This faith will be reinforced the first time you truly let go and allow and see how perfectly things work out without your interference.

Because we are so used to trying to *make* things happen—so used to our habits of controlling behavior—we may find that "allowing" has become somewhat foreign and must be relearned. It's the one element in choosing Easy World that can be a challenge, but I do believe you'll master this with practice. Just make it your intention and bring that intention to Easy World with you.

Breathe...Relax...Allow...Enjoy

ENJOY

Enjoyment is your reward for choosing Easy World, and it's also key to staying there. Pleasure is automatic when you enter EW and allow EW to do its magic on your behalf, because ease and joy are inseparable partners.

When you're enjoying, you are guaranteed that you're in Easy World, since enjoyment is a function of EW alone. You may have thought you'd experienced enjoyment in Difficult World, but if you were truly enjoying yourself, you had slipped into Easy World unawares! When the enjoyment ended, that's when you returned to Difficult World.

The "enjoy" part of the equation is not only a sign that you're there, but also a facilitator of staying in Easy World. By virtue of the Law of Attraction, the vibrational state you're in when you're experiencing joy is attractive to that which matches up with joy. Therefore, experiencing joy means you're creating more joy and ease. Joy begets joy.

AND WATCH THE MAGIC UNFOLD

There's actually one more element to the Easy World actions: ". . . and watch the magic unfold!" Once you're in Easy World, that's exactly what you're able to do! It's the instruction you'll usually find just after "Breathe . . . relax . . . allow . . . enjoy . . ." It was fed to me while I was designing the look of the Easy World Web site by the same intelligence that told me I needed to add the Easy World actions to the directions for getting to Easy World.

Breathe . . . Relax . . . Allow . . . Enjoy

This particular line played a key role in my being able to make it to Easy World at a time when I really needed to, so I've experienced its simple power.

Rick and I were driving home from our annual late-summer vacation at Lake Michigan when we encountered a gigantic electrical storm. (You'll be reading more about our Michigan trips. They seem to always call forth Easy World adventures— and storms!) It had been a very long day in the car, and we were really intent on getting to Omaha, Nebraska, where we had hotel reservations. Getting that far meant we'd have a shorter drive the next day (it's a 1,400-mile trip one way from our family cottage in Michigan to our house in Denver, and we split it into two days). We were taking a gamble on the hotel—the price was amazing and they allowed pets. It didn't have to be a palace, just clean and comfortable.

As we drove through western Iowa after dark, still about 120 miles from Omaha, we noticed a thunderstorm ahead in exactly the direction we were going. The closer we got, the more dramatic the scene. It was quite magnificent, with giant bolts of lightning filling the night sky. Sometimes they looked bundled together, with a half dozen or more hitting at the same time in the same spot. I'd never seen anything quite like it. The flashes lit the whole landscape, from south to north as far as we could see.

While my enlightened self was enjoying the majesty of it, my animal body and worrywart, fearful self were getting very, very tense as we headed directly into it. It was all I could do to stop myself from imagining tornadoes, flooding, and other storm-related disasters. To top it off, we were in a construction zone with six lanes winnowed down to two with two-way traffic, complete with tight barricades, big trucks, heavy rain, and poor visibility.

I invoked Easy World and decided to try gratitude and appreciation for the storm, for our safety, et cetera, and that helped greatly, but that primitive survival part of my brain just kept giving the danger signal, and my body got tenser by the minute. Though I wanted to be, I was just not in Easy World. I had been saying the EW invocation over and over, but it wasn't enough.

Just as I could feel myself really starting to clench up again in fear and resistance, we passed an elegant billboard (is that an oxymoron?) with a photo of a butterfly on it that said, "Watch the magic unfold!"

I was astonished! There, in the Iowa countryside, was the Easy World tagline! In smaller lettering at the bottom, it gave the dates for the new butterfly exhibit at the Omaha zoo. To everyone else, it may have been a promo for the exhibit, but to me, it was clearly a message from Easy World to remind me that it's not just saying the words that gets you into Easy World, but also the actions.

I had been in such intense resistance, I had forgotten to breathe, relax, allow, enjoy, and watch the magic unfold! After that divine nudge, I focused on the Easy World actions, and as I breathed out the stress and allowed the storm to rage without

Breathe...Relax...Allow...Enjoy

resistance, I was able to stay centered and calm and be authentically thrilled at the most amazing light show I'd ever witnessed. Not only that, we got to Omaha safely, and found a lovely hotel waiting for us—far more upscale than its price would indicate. I was back in Easy World!

WHEN TO INVOKE EASY WORLD

When do you choose Easy World? You can probably figure this one out, but just in case, I will clue you in: You invoke Easy World whenever things are not easy! Or not harmonious. If things are easy and harmonious, you're in Easy World. If things are hard or if the word "harmony" cannot be used to describe the state you're in, you're not.

We are so used to things being difficult, however, it's sometimes a "can't see the forest for the trees" situation, and we may not always immediately recognize the signs of being in Difficult World.

If you've got a knot in your stomach, you're not in Easy World. If you've got a headache, you're not in Easy World. If you feel like yelling at someone, you're not in Easy World. If you feel like crying but you're resisting it, you're not in Easy World.

Here is a list of more clues that you are outside of Easy World. If you are experiencing any of these emotions, or if you're just not joyful, it means you're in Difficult World. When you realize you're there, you need to say the EW invocation and do the EW actions ASAP to get yourself back to Easy World!

Breathe...Relax...Allow...Enjoy

- Tension
- Stress
- Struggle
- Anxiety
- Impatience
- Pushing
- Envy
- Jealousy
- Confusion
- Worry
- Anger
- Desperation
- Frustration
- Irritation
- Exasperation
- Road rage
- Resentment
- Discomfort
- Pessimism
- Helplessness
- Hopelessness
- A feeling of being overwhelmed
- Doubt that things are working out harmoniously
- A desire to control other people or situations
- Resistance of any kind

Breathe...Relax...Allow...Enjoy

THE LAW OF EASY WORLD

Now that you know how and when to access Easy World, I need to tell you about Easy World's only law so you'll be able to stay there: *Worry, strife, and struggle, in any form, are strictly prohibited.*

Violation of that law triggers immediate—and I do mean immediate—expulsion from Easy World. Worry, strife, and struggle (including any of the above-listed behaviors and states of being) deliver you straight to Difficult World! Those fear-based, Difficult World behaviors simply can't exist in Easy World. So if you're experiencing them, you know you're not in EW anymore.

But there are no cops in EW to enforce the law—the law is *self*-enforced. *Only you* can expel yourself from Easy World. No one else has that power.

You also get to decide the length of your own sentence, and you can move back into Easy World whenever you decide to drop the offending behaviors.

Reentry to EW is automatic when you release those Difficult World ways and simply *allow* things to be easy, the way they are designed to be. And you'll be happy to know that no matter how long you've been away from it, Easy World is instantly accessible when you allow yourself to move back into it.

If you find yourself expelled from Easy World and want to get back to it, just choose Easy World again. Say the magic words,

Breathe...Relax...Allow...Enjoy

"I choose to live in Easy World, where everything is easy," then breathe . . . relax . . . allow . . . enjoy . . . and you're back!

INSTANT EASY WORLD

Let me share another example of just how quickly this can work. I recently switched mobile phone service. I ordered it online, and soon received a much-needed new phone, which I charged for twenty-four hours. Easy enough. Once that was done, however, and it was time to actually *use* the phone, it dawned on me that I knew nothing at all about this new phone, and my heart sank to think of learning about it. (Sinking hearts—so *not* Easy World!)

The instruction book that came with the phone had seemed a little overwhelming upon my brief perusal of it when the phone arrived, and I sure didn't look forward to dealing with it. To top it off, I wasn't even sure where the manual had ended up once it had been moved off the table to clear the way for dinner the day the phone had come. Locating it would require a search. I will admit that I had claimed defeat before even trying, and felt resentful and mildly angry that I was going to need to interrupt my writing to deal with the *&#@% thing!

Needless to say, I was not in Easy World. Just moments before, I had been, but once I started thinking about the prospect of figuring out the phone and having to do something I'd found difficult in the past, I was suddenly back in Difficult World.

Breathe . . . Relax . . . Allow . . . Enjoy

(There's a hint about one of the myriad ways Difficult World sucks you into it in that last sentence!)

As I contemplated overcoming my resistance to searching for the manual and tackling it to at least figure out the basics, it occurred to me that I might be able to find instructions for the phone on the manufacturer's Web site. If so, maybe they would be laid out in a format that I would find easier to deal with and understand.

Aware that I was definitely not in the right realm to ensure success, I decided I'd better invoke Easy World before starting an online search. So I said, "I choose to live in Easy World, where everything is easy—even figuring out new phones," and took a deep breath.

At that very instant, before I could even finish exhaling, I heard the chime that sounds when I have new e-mail. When I looked up at my computer screen—I kid you not—there was a fresh e-mail just in from my new phone company with the subject line "About Your New Mobile Phone." Hmmm . . .

I clicked it open, and lo and behold, the e-mail contained a link to a page on their Web site with the heading "Getting Started with Your New Phone," which included a phone diagram and well-laid-out, very easy-to-grasp instructions on the basics of my new phone!

All I had to do was invoke Easy World, and what I needed was provided instantly and effortlessly.

Oh, how I *love* Easy World!

Breathe . . . Relax . . . Allow . . . Enjoy

KEEP ON CHOOSING EASY WORLD

Getting to Easy World is supremely easy when you apply the instructions. But don't let me mislead you into thinking that there's no challenge at all with *staying* in Easy World. Because you are habituated to Difficult World, you will more than likely find yourself popping back out of Easy World over and over again and returning to the familiar realm of struggle.

Heaven knows, I've experienced that phenomenon myself, as have all the other people I know of who have embraced Easy World so far! But with practice, staying in Easy World will get easier and easier. Just keep choosing it.

Even if you don't feel you could possibly get to Easy World from the state you're in, just say the invocation, take the Easy World actions, and see what happens. I'm willing to bet you'll be back in Easy World faster than you thought possible; back to the realm of ease, joy, and things getting done by magic—Easy World magic!

If you slip back out again, just do it again as many times as you need to. (If you are finding it just too, too much of a challenge to stay in Easy World, or if you feel you aren't getting there to start with, you may need to try some of the recommendations in Chapter 7, "Finding Easy World in the Dark.")

Truly, entering Easy World is as easy as you allow it to be. You simply need to remember to choose it—and *keep* choosing it as often as necessary. Whatever your challenge, Easy World

Breathe...Relax...Allow...Enjoy

will deal with it effortlessly, efficiently, and effectively, and by choosing Easy World, you'll get to experience that!

Now that you have the key and know how easy it is to move into Easy World, let's give your inner analyst a little mind candy.

✦

I choose to live in Easy World,

where everything is easy.

✦

Breathe...Relax...Allow...Enjoy

3

What *Is* Easy World?

*L*et me assure you right from the start that you really don't have to know much, or even anything, about Easy World for it to work for you. You just need to remember to choose it. But when something changes your life the way Easy World has mine—or someone *tells* you something is going to change your life like I'm telling you that choosing Easy World will—the natural human response is to want to understand it.

It amazed me that whenever I would say the EW mantra, "I choose to live in Easy World, where everything is easy," and relax, things just worked out amazingly and effortlessly. This was dramatically different—and so much easier—than any of the dozens of techniques I had come across and tried in the almost thirty years of my devoted spiritual journey. It was phenomenal,

Breathe...Relax...Allow...Enjoy

and my analytical mind began to ask questions about what Easy World really is, and how and why it works.

As I opened myself to understanding the phenomenon, the workings of Easy World began to reveal themselves to me in all their simple elegance and glory. Being the inveterate teacher I am, I started writing down my insights about Easy World to share with you. So, for the mollification of *your* inner analyst, and to jump-start your own inquiry into the nature of Easy World, I will now share with you my current understandings about the structure and tenets of Easy World.

My understanding of quantum physics is fairly skimpy, and though I am certain that science will someday be able to confirm what I've been shown by Spirit about the workings of Easy World, this is going to be more of a metaphysical explanation than a scientific one!

The Design for Harmony

Easy World, the remarkable realm where ease and joy prevail, is a reality framework—or, rather, *the* reality framework— within which everything works together effortlessly, seamlessly, and in the flow. It is the reality matrix that was put in place to support your total well-being and harmonious relationship with the Whole of Creation and its constituent parts.

It is the energy field within which you were meant to create your life. Another term I sometimes use for Easy World is the

"Design for Harmony," though the Design for Harmony is actually just the foundation for Easy World.

A powerful creator, you are *always* creating, and the type of energy field within which you create determines the nature of your creation. As a human being who has been given free will, you are always choosing, consciously or, till now, mostly unconsciously, which energy field or matrix to create within.

When you choose to be in the Easy World reality, and you create your life in alignment with it, what you create is an experience of the blissful peace that comes from everything operating in sync with everything else and things working out as if by magic. Magic, which is the label we put on the phenomenon of things happening effortlessly, is nothing special in Easy World—it is normal.

The more you choose to be in Easy World, relaxing and allowing the intelligent, benevolent forces that operate in the EW reality to work on your behalf, acting only when inspired and energized to, the more magical experiences you will have. *When you choose Easy World, magic becomes an everyday facet of life.*

In Easy World, the *only* requirement for receiving all that you need and desire is the *allowing* of it. Period. That does seem magical after a lifetime spent in Difficult World, doesn't it?

Easy World is characterized by a continual, overarching devotion to *wholeness* at every level. It is set up so that it constantly aligns everything within it with the continuous flow of intelligence and life force (aka *Love*) from Source, and perfectly coordinates all within it with every other aspect of the Whole of Creation.

The nature of Easy World is to heal, enhance, and enliven. When you're in Easy World, you're fully partaking of Life Force (Love), and your wholeness, vitality, joy, and total well-being are perpetually supported. The coherent nature of Easy World ensures that problems cannot possibly exist there. What Easy World does is unite, harmonize, and vitalize.

With the Design for Harmony undergirding Easy World, and continually harmonizing everything, it's not only that no problems can arise in Easy World but also that any problem you may have in Difficult World is brought to resolution there. Easy World's dynamics ensure that everything works out in peaceful, life-enhancing ways for all.

Every particle of and participant in Easy World is compatible with every other—and everything that occurs within EW harmonizes with everything, everyone, and every other occurrence within it. Easy World is set up so that all operating therein are continually prospered and supported in being at their peak of growth and well-being.

When you are in Easy World, you are automatically provided with all the information, energy, and motivation you need to take inspired action that is in harmony with the Whole. You are aligned with that which will support your well-being and the well-being of all. Likewise, everyone else in EW experiences this also.

Breathe...Relax...Allow...Enjoy

Your "Default Setting"

Easy World is immensely powerful and magnetic, and as long as you aren't resisting it, its attractive power will keep you firmly ensconced in it, and your experience of life will be characterized by ease. Notice, however, the qualifier: *as long as you aren't resisting it.* We'll go over the whys and wherefores of your resistance to EW as we go along.

Just know that Easy World is your "default matrix," the energy schematic you automatically return to when you aren't in Difficult World. An immense, powerful magnetic field, Easy World will always pull you into it if you allow it to. It truly is your natural state, and *when you relax your mind and body, you will reliably go back to Easy World.* Isn't that great to know?

In or Out—It Is, and Always Has Been, a Choice

Easy World has been in place since before the beginning of time. Though we have come to believe that hardship and struggle are simply an integral part of the Earth experience, Earth-life was not originally designed to be difficult. Actually, things were set up to be easy!

What we're calling "Easy World" is the original design for living on Earth. It is the energy schematic from which the first human beings operated, and their experience was that of Paradise. Until, that is, they opted out of it for the first time.

Breathe...Relax...Allow...Enjoy

If you are familiar with the story featured in the sacred literature of most major religions that tells of a beautiful garden where the residents lived in bliss and wanted for nothing, then you know something of Easy World. In these stories, all was idyllic and lovely, with everything one could possibly require being perfectly supplied, even before anyone could need or want it. Talk about easy!

As this archetypal story unfolds, all is harmonious and perfect until the residents of the garden make the choice to ignore the guidelines they've been given for maintaining their easy life, and do the one thing the Creator has clearly warned them against doing. The result is that they immediately find themselves in a different world—a world of pain, suffering, struggle, and strife. Thus, Difficult World is born.

We're going to talk about this event a bit more as we get a little farther into the book (and trust me, it is *not* your daddy's "Fall of Man" story!) because it is important for us to understand that what exiled the characters in the story from their easy life is the same thing that, to this day, continually invites us out of Easy World. And, more important, that we have the choice to decline that invitation. *We have the choice in every moment to be either in Easy World or in Difficult World.*

Breathe...Relax...Allow...Enjoy

Just Say No to Difficult World by Saying *Yes* to Easy World

One of my favorite personal Easy World experiences to date illustrates how Easy World is always masterfully arranging things to support our well-being and happiness, *even when the evidence might appear to the contrary.* It shows that, even when we are continuously being invited out of Easy World, the choice is always ours whether to answer the invitation or not.

In September 2007, Rick and I, plus our two dachshunds, were headed to Lake Michigan from our home in Denver. (This trip predates the one in Chapter 2.) We were more than ready for a totally relaxing two-week stay at my sister's wonderful old Victorian-era cottage that sits only a few dozen steps from the shore of the lake. My elderly dad, whom I see only a couple of times a year, was to be there at the other family cottage, and it was going to be great to spend some time with him also. We were thrilled to be going!

We were driving our low-mileage, very reliable Honda Odyssey van, which we'd had thoroughly checked over by our neighborhood mechanic the week before we embarked on the journey. We invoked Easy World and set out with high spirits, expecting only smooth sailing on our way. That is just what we experienced—until we came within a forty-five-minute drive of the room we had booked for our first night's stop in Atlantic, Iowa, at an economical, dog-friendly hotel.

Breathe...Relax...Allow...Enjoy

There, we met up with a huge, violent storm whose lightning strikes lit up the Iowa countryside as if it were daytime. As you know from my story in the last chapter, electrical storms—especially while on the road, and particularly while driving in heavy rain—are Difficult World triggers for me.

Though I was being called there, I made sure to stay aligned with Easy World, and managed to remain calm and relaxed. We were able to make it to the hotel without incident, even in the pouring rain, by driving slowly and oh-so-carefully. The skies fully opened up as soon as we arrived, and neither of us had ever experienced such a downpour.

Fortunately, we had spent the day in Easy World, where paying attention to your intuition is a natural part of things. Without realizing it would be our last chance to walk the dogs and fill up the van without getting drenched, we had stopped at a gas station just before we reached the intense part of the storm. When we got to the hotel in the midst of the deluge, the only real challenge was unpacking the stuff we needed from the car.

While I got the dogs and myself settled in the hotel room, Rick valiantly, and without complaint, endured the rain to bring in our things. Though he was soaked, he was not unhappy—he was in Easy World, too.

The storm had effectively stymied our plans to go into town to get dinner, but fortunately, the hotel had frozen pizzas for sale, and facilities for baking them. We were amazed at how delicious that pizza was because it seemed heaven-sent. (I *told*

Breathe...Relax...Allow...Enjoy

you Easy World is magic—when you're in it, even cheap pizza tastes great!) And the rain went on and on, with the storm seemingly stalled over Atlantic.

Our room had wireless Internet service, and we had our laptops with us, so I decided to check some weather sites, only to find that the storm indeed *had* stalled over the tiny town, dumping a record amount of rain in a very short time. The highway we'd come in on was now partially flooded and no longer passable. Good thing we'd arrived when we had. We had joked about a place in the state of Iowa, far from any large body of water, being named after an ocean—now we had a clue as to why!

I decided to look into the forecast for the next day, and was none too pleased to see that the storm that had accompanied us into Atlantic was taking exactly our route eastward, and was even predicted to turn north and move up the eastern shore of Lake Michigan precisely as we would be doing the next day.

Based on its speed, we would be catching up with the storm by lunchtime, and would most likely be driving in it the rest of the day. I caught myself starting to freak out. Driving in the rain just did not fit in with the Easy World scenario I had planned. At all.

Determined to reach the cottage by dark the next evening, I was equally determined *not* to spend time traveling in the rain. This looked like an impossible situation—one that I knew I could not possibly figure out or control at the level of my ordinary awareness. Only a higher intelligence would be able to manage these seemingly juxtaposed intentions.

Breathe...Relax...Allow...Enjoy

So I said, "Look. That simply will not work. We will *not* drive through the rain and lightning all day and we *will* be at the cottage tomorrow night. I give this to Easy World to handle!" And then I added the EW magic words: "I choose to live in Easy World, where everything is easy." Immediately I felt complete peace and fell asleep, quite sure that the problem would somehow be taken care of in Easy World.

When we awoke the next morning, it was a beautiful, sunny day, the only hints of the storm being some puddles in the hotel parking lot and steam rising off the highway. I gathered our stuff and walked the dogs while Rick packed the car, and we were right on time to leave according to the schedule we had set.

We had some coffee and mini-muffins in our room and planned to stop down the road for a more substantial breakfast. We were just over a hundred miles from the charming little town of Newton, Iowa, where we had stayed in the past and where we knew we could get a breakfast we'd like. So Rick went to take the last of the stuff to the van and I was ready to join him after making a final check of the room.

But our departure was to be delayed—the van wouldn't start. Fortunately, we hadn't yet checked out and there were hours to go before checkout time, so we went back to our hotel room and called AAA. We did not let this incident concern us. Clearly, we were being watched over. I mean, if you're going to have car trouble on the road, best to have a comfy place to wait it out! (*Definitely* Easy World.)

AAA sent someone out immediately, and our wait was only

Breathe...Relax...Allow...Enjoy

about twenty comfortable minutes, relaxing on the bed, watching TV. Assuming that all the water from the night before had caused the battery to fail, the guy that AAA sent simply gave us a jump, assuring us that the drive would charge the battery back up. So we set off toward Newton and breakfast.

As we drove the few miles off the interstate into the heart of Newton, we were disappointed to discover that the restaurant where we had eaten before had changed hands and didn't serve breakfast anymore. So we decided not to get food after all, but just to stop and stretch and give the dogs a chance to relieve themselves. We spotted the ideal shady place behind some commercial buildings where there was a wide swath of green up against a stand of trees, just perfect for a dog walk on a summer morning.

We pulled around to the back of one of the buildings and parked, took the dogs for a stroll, and got back in the van. Rick turned the key and . . . nothing. So we called AAA again, and they said someone would be on the way. They asked for our location, which we weren't sure of, so I walked around to the front of the building so we could tell them where to find us. I nearly fell on the ground laughing when I read the business's sign. In our quest for the right dog-walking spot, we had unwittingly parked directly behind an auto-parts store!

While we waited for help, I suggested to Rick that he might want to go in the store and scope out a new battery. So he set off to do that while I sat in the shade with the dogs and read a magazine. He came back with a new battery and tales of a

Breathe . . . Relax . . . Allow . . . Enjoy

charming, Mayberry-like encounter with the guys who worked
in the store. Clearly, we were in Easy World. Where better to
have parked in our situation?

When AAA finally arrived after an hour's wait, Rick, who is
a computer wizard but not at all proficient in anything relating
to cars, offered the guy fifteen dollars (all the cash he had in his
pocket) to install the new battery, which he gladly did. We were
soon back on the road, feeling very grateful. Even though we
were a little chagrined at being so far behind schedule, we had
stayed centered and at peace in Easy World, and had never allowed Difficult World to seduce us, despite its many invitations.

The rest of the day's trip went without a hitch. Our new battery worked perfectly, and we made amazing time. *Truly* amazing time! In fact, when I had first called my dad to tell him where
we were in eastern Iowa, it was already afternoon. With so far to
go, including through the usually clogged roads around Chicago
at rush hour, he had beseeched us to spend another night on the
road. He was certain we would be catching up with the storm at
any minute and that it would be really, really late when we got in.

But, oddly, we never did catch up with the storm. When
we'd stop to eat or get gas or walk the dogs, we'd notice puddles,
and occasionally, we'd have to run the wipers to clear the light
sprinkles from the tail end of the storm we seemed to be continuously right behind, but that was the only evidence of it. It
was a bit cloudy most of the way, but that worked to our advantage as it kept the van cooler and more comfortable than if
there'd been bright sun beating down.

Breathe...Relax...Allow...Enjoy

We had fun listening to the Garrison Keillor CDs Rick had checked out from the library and, in general, just experienced harmony and joy. And even though we hit Chicago during the Friday-afternoon rush, we had an amazingly easy time making our way through, and were on the other side almost before we knew it.

The trip between Chicago and the cottage flew by, and we arrived not long after the sun had set—*and* just after the storm had passed. When we called Dad to say we were there, he was incredulous that we could have covered that much ground in such a relatively short amount of time.

We had succeeded in staying in Easy World—in just allowing things to unfold—instead of getting caught up in the notion that things were going wrong. Because we had, everything had lined up for us to have an easy, fun, safe trip, without encountering the violent weather. If we had not been delayed leaving our hotel, and again in Newton, we certainly would have been driving in the storm most of the day.

Our powerful intention to get to our destination that evening, my insistence on good driving conditions, our invocation of Easy World, and my faith in Easy World to arrange things for us, plus our continual appreciation of Easy World, had saved the day. Despite all the delays, we had miraculously ended up at the cottage at the very time we had originally planned to be there before any of the "obstacles" had presented themselves! It was almost eerie—as if we had somehow slipped in and out of time. *Easy World is a magical realm.*

Breathe...Relax...Allow...Enjoy

Of course, this could have turned out much differently if we had allowed ourselves to be triggered into choosing Difficult World by all the things that appeared to be going wrong. I'm sure I don't have to tell you how stressful that trip could have been if we had not had faith in the power of Easy World. If we had gotten caught up in appearances and slid into Difficult World, it would not have been a story about Easy World magic, but a Difficult World story of angst and general unpleasantness.

Easy World is always supporting our highest possibilities for well-being, even when the evidence seems to be to the contrary. You can bank on it. No matter what is going on around you, just have faith in Easy World, trust the process, and relax. Instead of choosing Difficult World out of fear and doubt, keep choosing Easy World no matter what, and you will reap the results of Easy World's amazing problem-solving power!

The Easy World Channel

Yes, believe it or not, you have been *choosing* Difficult World over and over and over again when you could have chosen Easy World! Doesn't it make you want to slap your forehead like they do in the classic TV commercial for the vegetable juice and say, "I could have had Easy World!"?

But just because we have continually opted out of Easy World and in to Difficult World by virtue of the choices we've made throughout our lives, thus keeping our focus and experi-

Breathe...Relax...Allow...Enjoy

ence in Difficult World, that doesn't mean that Easy World is any less available and accessible to us. It is, and always has been, operating on our behalf.

Easy World is holding steady with the same awesome power as in the beginning. It still provides the powerful matrix for harmony and effortlessness, where universal forces are working together on your behalf to support your well-being. And Easy World is always available—always a breath away. *Always.* Does knowing that thrill you as much as it does me?

Things are, and always have been, working out perfectly and with ease in Easy World, whether we are aware of it or not. But you have to *be* in the EW reality in order to experience that perfect outworking.

Easy World is a wholly different reality, and what is occurring within it cannot be perceived from Difficult World. When you're in Easy World, it doesn't matter what is going on in Difficult World because something entirely different is occurring in Easy World.

They are like two TV stations operating at distinctly different frequencies. You can't see what's happening on Channel 1 if you have the set tuned to Channel 2* (Easy World is definitely

---

*Disclaimer: The designations of Channel 1 and Channel 2 are not intended in any way to imply that actual television channels with those numbers are correlated with Easy World and Difficult World, respectively! There is no implication whatever that a real TV entity named Channel 2 is somehow bad! It is only to denote that Easy World is the realm of oneness, and Difficult World is the realm of duality ("two-ness" or "more-than-one-ness"). Heck, I've very much liked the Channel 2's I've encountered in my TV-watching lifetime!

Breathe...Relax...Allow...Enjoy

Channel 1!) and vice versa. To better understand this, let's imagine that you're watching TV and there's wrestling on one channel and a nature program on another. If you're watching the wrestling program, you can't see what's happening on the nature program.

You simply cannot experience the harmony and splendor of Easy World if you are tuned in to Difficult World. So even though things are working out perfectly for you in EW, if you are in DW, you won't have that as your experience.

If you are drawn into Difficult World through such fear-based mental activities as worrying, trying to control things, judging, or being disappointed about the way things seem to be unfolding, et cetera, you'll be in the wrong reality to experience the harmonious outworking of whatever it is you desire. For ease and harmony, you must have your dial set to Easy World.

You can move in and out of EW at the flip of a mental switch, just like you can toggle between two stations on the TV with one little button on the remote control. But why would you leave Easy World? Well, keeping your tuner set to the EW channel would be super easy if there wasn't an aspect of your being that adamantly preferred Channel 2. We'll get to that soon.

HIGH-VIBE EASY WORLD

The idea about Easy World and Difficult World being at two different frequencies is not simply metaphorical. Easy World indeed exists at a higher vibrational frequency than Difficult

Breathe...Relax...Allow...Enjoy

World. If you're new to the idea of everything being energy and of energy vibrating at different rates or frequencies, here is a quick, and admittedly oversimplified, primer:

At the center or core of Creation is Source, the origin of all energy. This is where energy vibrates the fastest; it's the aspect of Creation demonstrating the highest vibrational frequency of all. At this level, there is no impediment whatsoever to the flow of Life Force out from the core. Energy/Life Force/Love, and the intelligence encoded within it, radiates freely and ceaselessly from Source. You might say that energy flows with perfect *ease.*

The Divine Intelligence operating at Source level creates worlds, and every nuance of those worlds, but *experiences no effort whatsoever in doing so.* This is because it is doing so from a state of total nonresistance.

Are you familiar with the Creation story in the Book of Genesis in the Bible? Genesis I, verse 3, says, "And God said, 'Let there be light,' and there was light." *Let* there be light! No effort—God simply *allowed* light, and light showed up! Instantly! Now, *that's* manifestation, *that's allowing*, at the highest level! Needless to say, the Creator is 100 percent Easy World!

The more Love you allow to flow freely through you, the higher you go in vibrational frequency. The higher you go in vibrational frequency, the more your experience matches that of Source: perfect ease and instantaneous manifestation of desires. The lower you go in vibrational frequency, the more difficult and painful your experience will be and the more challenging and time-consuming it will be to manifest your desires.

Breathe...Relax...Allow...Enjoy

The aspects of Creation that allow energy to flow freely stay at the highest vibrational frequency possible, according to their unique design, and experience total health, wholeness, and, of course, ease. This is the state of those in Easy World.

The aspects of Creation that *resist* the flow of energy from Source experience varying degrees of stress and deterioration. Resistance to the flow of Love/Life Force from Source is how Difficult World is created. In Difficult World, there is resistance—sometimes massive resistance—to the flow, and thus, a lack of ease, a lack of wholeness, a lack of joy.

So, basically, if you prefer not to experience pain, difficulty, and stress, and you want to experience ease, well-being, and joy, then you want to allow a free flow of Love through you so you can be at higher vibrational frequency. That is where you find Easy World, where everything is easy.

As the cherry on top, as if ease were not enough, higher vibrational frequency is what catalyzes your emotional response of joy. Ease and joy are inseparable partners. Where there is one, you will always find the other. Joy is the sign that you are at higher vibrational frequency. You might say that joy is the emotional signature of Easy World.

CONSCIOUSLY CHOOSING EASY WORLD

Whenever you've experienced joy, you've been in Easy World, however briefly. You've dropped resistance and allowed yourself to be drawn back into the magnetic field of the Design for

Breathe...Relax...Allow...Enjoy

Harmony. In addition to experiencing joy, I'm sure you've experienced things working out really easily and harmoniously without having *consciously* chosen Easy World.

My guess is that these things happened when you were relaxed—perhaps in a playful mood or totally absorbed in an activity, and just enjoying yourself, not stressing out about anything. You were not obsessing, not trying to "push the river," or to make things go a certain way. You were just naturally allowing the flow. You were choosing Easy World spontaneously without realizing it. These are the joyful moments that we live for and long for when we are in Difficult World.

Now, instead of having the Easy World experience be something that seems to occur purely by grace, you can choose this at will.

As you learned in Chapter 2, you can say the EW invocation: "I choose to live in Easy World, where everything is easy." Then breathe, relax, allow, and enjoy. It is no coincidence at all that the actions you take to move yourself fully into the embrace of Easy World are chief among the ones I recommend when someone asks me how she can raise her vibrational frequency! (You'll be learning more about frequency-raising techniques in Chapter 7.)

Breathe...Relax...Allow...Enjoy

If Channel 1 Is Where All the Joy Is, Why in the World Would I Choose Channel 2?

There's a part of you that is hooked on Channel 2. This part is a Difficult World addict! It thrives in Difficult World, and in Difficult World only. Its very existence depends upon keeping you in DW, focused on Channel 2. It is the producer, director, and programming executive for Channel 2. It needs you to be both actor and audience, which, of course, requires that it keep you out of Easy World. It is really excellent at its job.

When we get to Chapter 5, we'll learn more about this very ambitious entity and how to override it so as to keep tuned to Channel 1, the EW channel. In the next chapter, though, I'll introduce the amazing you—the biggest part of you, actually—that keeps the home fires burning in Easy World.

I choose to live in Easy World,

where everything is easy.

Breathe...Relax...Allow...Enjoy

4

Your Personal Easy World Guide

hether you find yourself in Easy World or Difficult World is determined by who has control of the clicker. There is one aspect of you that is always tuned in to Channel 1, and then there is the aspect of you that absolutely has a thing for Channel 2 and takes every opportunity to grab the remote so it can shift your focus to the inharmonious reality it prefers.

You are the one who decides who has control of the clicker at any given time.

Before I introduce you to the aspect of you that prefers Difficult World, I think it will be heartening to know that the vast majority of your being—what I call your *Spirit,* or your Self with a capital "S"—is constantly in Easy World, and continuously inviting you into it. Orienting to this exalted aspect of yourself is a surefire way to orient yourself to Easy World.

Breathe...Relax...Allow...Enjoy

You and Your Spirit

You are multifaceted and so much larger than you may be aware. Your ordinary waking consciousness and personality are just the tip of the iceberg. What you have probably been considering to be "you" is not the largest part of you, nor the highest in vibration, nor the most aware. Actually, the largest definition of "you" encompasses as much as you are willing to believe and allow! As far up the vibrational scale as you can go, you will find your Self there.

But for the purposes of this discussion, let's simply consider that there is what you perceive as the human you, and what you perceive as the Spirit of you. Your Spirit is the interface between your ordinary, ego-influenced self and your infinite Self—the Self that is one with and inseparable from Source. Just as an electrical outlet serves as your interface between the plug of the appliance you want to supply electricity to and the main power plant, so your Spirit is your interface with the infinite higher levels of Source energy and Divine Intelligence. And, of course, with Easy World.

Always in Easy World

Your Spirit is perpetually operating in Easy World. It is a permanent resident, and it never leaves. It is never seduced out of Easy World and the Design for Harmony—ever. Even when

Breathe...Relax...Allow...Enjoy

you are experiencing Difficult World, your Spirit is completely ensconced in Easy World.

While you may go "unconscious" and drift back to Difficult World, you can be assured that your Spirit never does. It is always fully attuned with the Design for Harmony, and orchestrating events to promote your ultimate well-being. This is true even when you are completely unaware of it and not feeling a connection with your Spirit.

You're never truly separated from your Spirit, but you can move vibrationally to a space where you are unaware of it. You can become polarized to other influences so that your Spirit's intelligence is not steering your experience, and when this happens, you are in Difficult World.

You are always in Easy World when you are allowing your Spirit to navigate, and always in Difficult World when you are not. You have free will to stay within the embrace of your Spirit and follow its guidance or not, and thus, to be in the embrace of Easy World or not to be.

When you invoke Easy World, and relax and allow yourself to be pulled into alignment with it, you are allowing yourself to be reunited with your Spirit. Just like Easy World is your "default reality," the one you always go back to when you relax and stop resisting its powerful magnetic draw, your Spirit is there, always waiting with open arms to embrace you when you allow yourself to be embraced.

Breathe...Relax...Allow...Enjoy

WHO WOULD YOU PREFER TO
HAVE STEWARDING YOUR LIFE?

You get to choose, ultimately, whether your Love-embodying, joy-inducing Spirit or your Difficult World–preferring, pain-mongering, fearful self is going to determine what you experience.

A magician in the highest and truest sense, your Spirit has the power to arrange events and situations so that they serve your ultimate well-being, as well as the ultimate well-being of everyone else. Whatever you need, your Spirit knows it. And arranges delivery of it. *Your Spirit is always working things out perfectly for you in Easy World.* Sounds like someone whose guidance you'd be willing to follow, doesn't it?

Believe me when I tell you that it's not just some airy-fairy mystical practice to honor your Spirit as your guide—it's supremely practical! Would you prefer that the navigator of your life be a limited facet of the human mind that is fearful and not very bright and bases its shortsighted agenda on something other than what is ultimately right and harmonious for you, *one that thrives as long as it can keep you in Difficult World?* Or would you rather rely on your unlimited Spirit, who is divine and all-knowing, all-seeing, with your highest possibilities for your well-being and happiness as its priority?

Another great advantage to allowing your Spirit to be in charge is that, because it is interfaced with the overall Design

Breathe...Relax...Allow...Enjoy

for Harmony and with the Spirit of every other being, the perfect outworking of events it is orchestrating for you is always
exactly in alignment with the highest possibilities for everyone
and everything else as well. That's the beauty of allowing an
omniscient and omnipotent intelligence to be in charge!

Making sure you keep the remote in the hands of your Spirit
assures you of having an Easy World life that is harmonious
and joyful. The more you consciously align with your Spirit, the
more you will naturally dwell in Easy World. When you honor
your Spirit as the guiding star for your life, have faith in its
continual arrangement of things to support your well-being
and joy, and deliberately choose for it to be in charge of your
reality and experience, you empower Easy World as your desired reality.

How I Fell in Love with My Spirit

There have been times in my life that I've been so out of alignment, so mired in Difficult World and feeling so powerless, I've
had no choice but to take my hands completely off the wheel
and say, "*You* drive!" And things have worked out amazingly.
Magically, even. I've approached difficult situations both ways,
and it is absolutely more empowering to stay in conscious com-
munion with my Spirit and to trust that I, at a limited, personality level, do not have to be in charge, and indeed am better
off when I'm not!

I've been relying on my Spirit with amazing results for quite

Breathe...Relax...Allow...Enjoy

a long time. Even my evidence-addicted fearful self has to grudgingly admit that things always work out when I put my total trust there—it still resists doing that, but it can't deny that it always works.

The first time I experienced the power of handing a problem over to my Spirit was back in 1982, and it was a doozy of a situation. An American citizen from North Carolina, I was overseas, teaching art in an international school in Japan, far from family and friends, when I found myself facing the challenge of a lifetime: I was diagnosed with a chronic, medically incurable, debilitating, and exceedingly painful autoimmune disease.

It had come upon me with a vengeance and was rapidly taking a toll. Some months after the diagnosis, I discovered I had become physically addicted to one of the drugs I had been prescribed—a corticosteroid—and that it was just as harmful as the disease itself. It was already causing me problems.

While I'd been in denial at first, not wanting to face the certain doom ahead of me that the doctor had described, I was suddenly catapulted into learning all I could about the disease and the drug. It was pretty dismal. I then set about getting off the steroids, visiting specialist after specialist in search of the answer. Even a weeklong stay at the clinic of a renowned specialist who had done all he could to rapidly wean me off them had been a failure.

The first information to give me hope came in the form of a book sent by a friend from home. I was thrilled to read that

Breathe...Relax...Allow...Enjoy

despite modern medicine's failure to deal effectively with the disease, the holistic approach promoted by this book had wrought remarkable results. The book made everything in me shout "YES!" when it talked of the innate power within to heal as long as the impediments to healing were removed. This seemed like the truest of truths to me. The toxic medications I was taking were definitely classified as impediments, and the book confirmed my intuition that they were making things worse.

It was as if I had been handed a reprieve from the gallows as I felt the excitement rising within me. I just knew I would find a way to follow this program. I would get off the meds, and emerge from the nightmare I found myself in. And then, my high hopes were dashed in an instant, as I read that the only way this approach would *not* work was if one had been on corticosteroids—the very class of drug I was having such a dickens of a time withdrawing from—for a protracted period. I'd been on a high dosage for seven months.

This was a crushing blow. Nothing the so-called experts had offered me had helped me—in fact, most of it had actually made things worse. There wasn't a medicine or an allopathic protocol recommended at that time for this illness that hadn't been tried, and yet my health just continued to decline.

If the holistic way to deal with it was closed to me, what was I going to do? I had run out of options. The doctors had warned me that I was heading for complete disability, and at the rate things were progressing, it would come sooner rather than later. And things were pretty awful already.

Breathe...Relax...Allow...Enjoy

I was at my wit's end, which I now know is an immensely powerful place to be, but at the time, it seemed like the weakest possible position to be in. With all the conventional approaches exhausted, and the one real alternative appearing to be out of the question, I had what was for me a very new feeling: utter despair.

I had always managed to end up on top when dealing with challenges. I'd prided myself on my ability to dig deep and emerge the victor in any difficult situation, and I'd felt I could handle anything life threw at me. But this was different. After doing all I knew to do, I'd hit a dead end. Suddenly, my whole future—and my present—was on the line, and I did not see a lifeline in sight.

But there was one place I had not yet looked.

As the futility of the situation crashed in on me, my fear and frustration turned to anger, and I began to yell and scream about the unfairness of it all. The yelling morphed into crying, and then the loud sobs turned into wailing. As my energy dissipated, the wailing became keening, and then it happened.

A little child's voice coming from somewhere within me called out, "Help me."

"Help me, help me, help me, help me," the small voice cried over and over, as if certain that someone would come to the rescue, though there wasn't another human being within earshot. As the pleas faded, so with them went all the residual fear energy, and what was left was stunning: the peace that passes understanding. Though nothing about my situation had outwardly changed, everything was completely different.

Breathe...Relax...Allow...Enjoy

It was as if the sun had come out and filled the sky with light after days on end of dark clouds. I felt amazingly good. I still had no answers; no new plan to pursue. But I was, oddly, at peace, with no fear of what lay ahead—indeed, I had a strange sense of well-being for someone who had no idea how she was going to solve her problems and who thought she was doomed to a living hell. I went to bed then, and slept more soundly than I had in . . . well, ever.

In the morning when I awoke, I still felt wonderful, and as I got ready to go to school, I got out all the medicines I was still taking. As I was about to down yet another handful of what I now considered to be poison—but necessary poison until I could find an alternative—I said something of a prayer: "Please show me how to protect my body from these toxic drugs until I can wean myself off them!"

That afternoon, as I reported for duty to the classroom of the biology teacher, who served as yearbook co-adviser with me, the high-school kids on the yearbook staff crowded around me to ask permission to go take photos, to get page layout approvals, and to attend to the other bits of business that needed to be attended to.

All the while I was interacting with them, my attention was being pulled to a book that was at the other end of the long lab table at which I was holding court. Though I had no idea what it was, I felt the large, dark-colored volume calling to me and, like a powerful magnet, pulling me to it.

As soon as the kids' needs were handled, I wasted not a

Breathe . . . Relax . . . Allow . . . Enjoy

second going to see what it was. It was called *The Encyclopedia of Common Diseases.* Interestingly, it was by the same publisher as the book that my friend had sent me: the one that had given me so much hope and that had dashed that hope as well.

Intrigued, I picked up the book and opened it at random. Remarkably, I opened it to the very section that pertained to my own health challenge. I turned a couple of pages, and the hairs on my arms stood up. Right there in black and white was a section on nutritional buffers for the commonly prescribed medications for this disease. All the ones I was on were listed! I was stunned and incredulous.

I called out to my fellow teacher, whose classroom it was, and said, "Where did this book come from?"

He said, "The school library—I was just browsing after lunch today, and it looked interesting. If you want to, take it. I don't even really know why I checked it out since we don't cover the human body till next semester."

I sure knew why! It was the answer to the plea I'd uttered that very morning. The list of nutritional supplements to protect my body from the medications was clearly the answer to my spontaneous prayer. Not only that, I knew that it, and the feeling of being miraculously taken care of, was in response to the small child's "Help me" cries from the night before.

Without fully understanding what I was doing, I had dropped my burdens, allowed myself to come into alignment, and asked my Spirit for help, and now I was getting it—in record time, and in

an amazing way! There was no mistaking the connection between what I had asked for and what I had received.

I knew then and there I had moved into a new reality, though
I might not have known what to call it. Now I would call it Easy
World; then I simply knew it as a different way of being—one
in which you asked for what you needed and it was given immediately and with perfect ease. A place of miracles!

And the miracles did not stop there. I continued surrendering to my Spirit, and within only a few months, my personal
Easy World guide had arranged for me to wean myself from the
drugs, had delivered me to health again, and had guided me to
an amazing experience of cosmic consciousness. The foundation of what you are reading in this book, and that of my first
book, *Recreating Eden*, all developed from that. And it all came
from surrendering to my Spirit, and letting it, alone, lead me.

THE MOST INFAMOUS EXIT
FROM EASY WORLD

As I was writing *Recreating Eden,* I was led, almost against my
will, to study the first few chapters of the Book of Genesis.
What I was guided to see is the present-day relevance of the
story of Adam and Eve and the Garden of Eden.

Here's the thing: Despite what you may have heard about that
story, despite how it's been abused and used to support some
pretty bizarre ideas like male superiority, women being the root

of all problems, sex being dangerous and bad, snakes being evil, et cetera; despite the common notion that it is a story about human beings being doomed forever, that is not what I was guided to see it being about at all. Basically, it's about how we first left Easy World, and it shows us how we keep on leaving it!

Not only that, it provides the key to getting *back* to Easy World.

This is not just a story found in the Judeo-Christian tradition; versions of it can be found in the sacred literature of most of the major religions and wisdom traditions on the planet. It is one of humanity's master stories—perhaps *the* master story for humanity—and like any master story, it conveys multiple ideas, layered one over another, and can be interpreted in many ways, some of them constructive and true to the intent of the story, some of them not. For our purposes, we're going to consider the story in light of what it says about being in Easy World and being out of Easy World.

In a nutshell, the protagonists of the story, Adam and Eve, were living in a pristine world of great beauty, abundant supply, and total harmony that fully supported their well-being. (Does this sound familiar?) They had no worries, and everything was provided for them as they simply enjoyed their glorious existence.

An eternal experience of ease and joy was theirs—all they had to do was obey one simple rule, which was to refrain from doing one forbidden thing. Doing this thing, they were told by the creator and provider of all this bounty, would cause them to be evicted from their ideal world.

Breathe...Relax...Allow...Enjoy

Without even going into what the thing was that they were to avoid doing,* I want to make the point here that their creator and provider of all—we'll call this creator/provider "Spirit"—spelled out the guidelines for staying in their perfect world of abundance and bliss, and they violated those guidelines. What happened?

The story says a serpent seduced them into doing the very thing they had been told would lead to disaster. Essentially, they listened to and acted on a voice—an influence—other than that of Spirit. Suddenly, they found themselves locked out of the garden, their perfect world of ease. For the first time, they experienced pain, suffering, and hardship. They found themselves in Difficult World.

Bottom line: Listen to and obey Spirit's guidance, and you'll be in Easy World. Listen to the other voice and do as it says, and you'll find yourself in Difficult World.

Whose was the other voice? What does the serpent represent? It belongs to the "Difficult World Dictator" (DWD), which we will be focusing on in the next chapter. The symbolism of the serpent relates to the primitive aspect of the human brain that runs the DWD's program.

This is an age-old story that is as current today as when it was first told. The exact same principles apply: If you want to stay in Easy World, don't let any voice override your Spirit's voice. Honor your Spirit's guidance and don't listen to the serpent. *Don't let the Difficult World Dictator seduce you.*

---

*This is thoroughly discussed in *Recreating Eden*.

Breathe...Relax...Allow...Enjoy

But How Do I Know Who's Who?

How can you tell the difference between guidance from your Spirit and a seduction from the DWD?

First and foremost, when guidance comes from your Spirit, it's always accompanied by an increase of Love and a feeling of expansiveness and greater openness in your body, especially in your heart center. When you're in alignment with your Spirit, you'll be encouraged to embrace, accept, and allow. That which is coming from your Spirit is encouraging, uplifting, and joyful. When the fearful ego is in charge, it's just the opposite.

Messages from Spirit are elegantly simple. That's not the case with messages from the DWD, who vastly prefers complication and complexity. Though they certainly can, rarely do messages from Spirit come in sentences; nor are they often verbal. They present in bursts of insight, in symbols and visions, in feelings, and, probably most often, simply in a general *knowing*.

Once you are fully aligned with your Spirit, you will not even notice the transmissions as being messages at all, but simply as what you are inspired to do or understand. Your thoughts will be your Spirit's thoughts and vice versa.

Ideally, you will become so aligned with your Spirit—so at one with it—that you will be a full-time resident of Easy World. At this point, I know that's a bit of a stretch. And you may not even think you'd want to be. But the more closely you align with your Spirit, the more you'll be in Easy World, the more authentic power you'll wield, and the more fulfilled you'll be.

Breathe...Relax...Allow...Enjoy

At this point, of course, any concern you may have about whether or not you'd like to live in Easy World full-time is rather moot! Until you understand how the Difficult World Dictator works, why he[*] is so desperate to keep you out of Easy World, and how to neutralize his attempts to change the channel and pull you into DW, you are in little danger of becoming a full-time Easy World resident. In reality, you'll probably be spending more time than you'd like with your dial set to Channel 2.

So, now that you know about your personal Easy World guide, let's learn more about the nature of the clicker-hogging Difficult World bully-dictator, and what *his* voice sounds like. Let's find out the only effective way to handle him.

I choose to live in Easy World,

where everything is easy.

---

[*] I'm using male pronouns for the Difficult World Dictator because this aspect of you, whether you are a male or female human being, utilizes your left-brain, inner masculine energy. This is not at all intended to be an insult to the male gender!

Breathe...Relax...Allow...Enjoy

5

Introducing the Difficult World Dictator

aaaahhh, Easy World. Blissful, peaceful, prosperous, Love-filled Easy World. Who would not love it? Well, believe it or not, as wonderful as Easy World is, there is an aspect of you—and of me—that is deathly afraid of it, that absolutely can't stand it, and that is committed to doing everything in its power to keep us out of it.

This entity always wants us to be in Difficult World instead. Every time it gets the remote—and it's always grabbing for it—it changes the channel to the Difficult World channel. Every chance it gets, it pulls you back into its preferred realm of struggle, strife, and complication.

Why? This entity's purpose—its very raison d'être—is to keep you in the only reality where it has any power. It does all it can to keep you where it can get its needs met, regardless of

Breathe...Relax...Allow...Enjoy

the fact that the majority of you is not at all happy or fulfilled there. It does not care that being in Difficult World is frustrating for you—it feeds off your frustration! Basically, it eats your unhappiness for dinner and relishes it (all the while pretending it wants you to be happy).

This character continually cons you into thinking that it is going to deliver what you desire, but it really can't, and doesn't even actually want to. It is always leading you to frustration, disappointment, turmoil, and pain, because that is the energy it needs to survive. If your desires were to be fulfilled and you were satisfied and happy, it would be out of a job—heck, it would be out of existence!

We'll call this entity the Difficult World Dictator because he creates, sustains, and ruthlessly rules Difficult World through deceit, trickery, and manipulation. He does so at the expense of your ease and joy.

Totally committed to keeping you in the difficult realm he rules, the DWD is loath to have light shined upon him lest you become wise to his tricks and choose to override his influence. Because this book is devoted to helping you do just that, if you're feeling any resistance to reading it, you now know why! Your inner Easy World–phobe is trying to keep you from knowing there is an option other than Difficult World.

Indeed, if you doubt the existence of Easy World, it is because this part of you desperately needs to keep you from choosing it. It is carrying on an age-old campaign of disinformation to be sure that you don't even *know* about Easy World, or, if you do

Breathe...Relax...Allow...Enjoy

happen to learn about it, that you are too sophisticated to fall for something so naive, simplistic, and "too good to be true."

Difficult World's Desperate Dependent

To be fair, it's a survival issue. It's not that this aspect is against you; it's that without Difficult World, it doesn't even exist. DW is the only reality in which it does. It's the only world it knows. So, it does its best to keep you out of Easy World because it not only has no power or control there, it is a complete nonentity. In Easy World, only the aspects of you that are willing to align with the Design for Harmony, to allow Love to flow freely, and to embrace joy exist. That does *not* describe this part of your psyche!

No, this aspect is joyless, paranoid, completely resistant to the flow of Love, and always on the lookout for reasons to be critical, angry, and frustrated. Its loftiest state seems to be mild disgruntlement; occasionally, it will soar for a moment when it finds a reason to gloat.

It is really quite comfortable with pain and failure, even while it squawks and cries crocodile tears about how unfair everything is and deceives you about who and what is to blame for your misery.

Breathe...Relax...Allow...Enjoy

Who Is That Difficult World Devotee, Anyway?

What is this contrary part of you commonly called? (And rest assured, all of us have one—it's not just *you* that's got this wack-job entity within!) What is another name for the Difficult World Dictator? Its common name is "ego."

Because there are multiple facets of ego, I'm going to refer to the DWD as the *"fearful* ego." That pretty much sums up the version of ego I'm talking about. Yes, as a human being, having an ego is a necessity, but there are some facets of the human ego that have just gotten carried away and have overstepped their bounds—that definitely includes the fearful ego.

Fearful. Full of fear. That is a perfect description of ego as the Difficult World Dictator. Fear is a distrust of Love. It's a distrust of the Design for Harmony. Your fearful self doesn't "get" Easy World, where Love flows freely, the Design for Harmony reigns, and things are always working together to support your highest possibilities for well-being, *at all.*

Liar, Liar, Pants on Fire

Your fearful ego is a Difficult World addict, and like any addict, he does not hesitate to spin things however he has to in order to get his fix. He is a consummate liar—he is *the* liar. In

Breathe...Relax...Allow...Enjoy

fact, deception is the very foundation of his existence and his primary technique for getting his needs met.

You can be absolutely certain that if the Difficult World Dictator tells you something, it is a big fat lie. Because the foundation of his existence is the Design for *Dis*harmony, he's a complete natural at it. From *his* viewpoint, he's telling the truth. But it's only true in Difficult World. *A Difficult World truth is always a lie!*

The Difficult World Dictator is slick. He deceives you continuously to suck you into his plans for getting what he needs. He tells you things like "You're running out of money" to scare you so that he can feast off your fear. Or he says, "You're worthless" so he can feed off your pain. Neither of these things is actually true.

The truth is that the universe is infinitely loving and abundant, and you always have access to that bounty in Easy World. And worthless? You are *so* valuable that no one can take your place! You are a one-of-a-kind expression of Source energy—of Love—and without you, Creation would be incomplete. Whenever the DWD tells you something, you can be sure the truth is really the opposite.

Anything less than loving that you hear in your head is coming from this desperado, who is charged with keeping you out of Easy World. Indeed, anything unloving you hear from *anyone* originates with this entity, who is duty-bound to perpetuate Difficult World at all costs—and you pick up the tab. You pay with your misery.

Breathe...Relax...Allow...Enjoy

THE DWD'S BIG BAG OF LIES AND TRICKS

The Difficult World Dictator has a seemingly bottomless bag of lies and tricks to keep you where he wants you. Here are just a few of them:

> DWD LIE: If you just resist something strongly enough, it will go away.

Resistance is the crown jewel in the DWD's repertoire, the foundation for everything he does. It is his *power,* and the more of your being he can enlist in resisting, the more fulfilled he is.

The more you'd prefer something *not* be in your life, the more you'd prefer not to be experiencing something, the more the DWD goads you to resist it. But when you resist something—anything—you simply strengthen its presence in your experience. The more you resist, the greater the power of that which you are resisting becomes in your life!

When you resist anything, you're resisting Easy World. The very act of resisting puts up a barrier to the flow of Love, which then drops your vibrational frequency and moves you into Difficult World, where everything you *don't* want to have in your experience figures prominently! Pretty nifty trap, huh?

If the DWD has his way, your knee-jerk reaction to anything that's going on in your life that you wish was not will be to resist. But if, instead, you choose Easy World and relax and *allow,* the thing you don't want will evaporate! Being in Easy World means

Breathe...Relax...Allow...Enjoy

you are aware only of that which is consistent with your joy. When you're tuned in to Channel 1, the irritations of Channel 2 don't even exist.

DWD LIE: Struggle and sacrifice lead to happiness.

The Difficult World Dictator has long championed the idea that somehow, struggle adds value to your endeavors, and that working hard is noble. He insists that pushing hard, struggling, and sacrificing happiness in the moment will pay off in a bonanza of joy and fulfillment later.

The notion that you must sublimate your true talents and passions to suck it up and do whatever seems to be required in order to survive or to get ahead supports Difficult World by keeping you frustrated and unfulfilled. The Difficult World concepts "Like it or not, you just gotta do what you gotta do to survive" and "If I sacrifice now, I'll be happy later," though lies, can certainly *seem* very real.

Remember, you create your reality according to your beliefs, so if you buy into these false ideas, you then create evidence to support them. And evidence is king to your logic-oriented left brain. That is how the illusion that is Difficult World is continually being created and sustained. The DWD convinces us of something and we create our experiences accordingly. Pretty soon, there's a whole world of evidence to support the lies.

I can just imagine that you might right now be thinking,

Breathe...Relax...Allow...Enjoy

"But working hard is so satisfying! I'm proud of what I've worked hard and struggled and sacrificed for. Besides, only deadbeats are unwilling to work hard." That's exactly what the DWD wants you to believe.

But think: Was it really how *hard* you worked that is the point of pride? Or was it that you dug down into your inner reserves and persevered *despite* how hard it was? Is the achievement really in the struggle? Or is it in *surviving* the struggle, achieving a goal, and emerging into a more peaceful, easy, joyful place?

Let me be very clear here: There are few things as satisfying and uplifting as being passionately, intensely engaged in challenging activity. That may be what some categorize as "hard work," but that's not hard at all. That's Easy World! *My* definition of hard work is when you're doing something that's draining your energy; something you're not cut out for; something that doesn't flow for you; *something that feels like a struggle.*

Struggle is so very Difficult World. The path to joy is in Easy World. And it's not a very long path at all. You simply choose Easy World, and you're experiencing joy! Ease and joy are constant companions. Difficulty and joy do not even know one another; they exist on different planes. You truly cannot access happiness in Difficult World, and the only way that struggling can lead to joy is when you stop!

DWD LIE: Before you can have what you desire, you need to deserve it.

Breathe...Relax...Allow...Enjoy

The concept of deserving was devised by the Difficult World Dictator to keep you from allowing the free flow of Love and abundance. From the standpoint of Source, the provider of all, everyone has equal rights to everything, no matter what he or she has done or hasn't done. There is no judgment of worthiness. At the Source level, there is no judgment at all!

Source continuously flows abundance, and the one and only thing that determines if you receive it is whether or not you're *allowing* yourself to. You don't have to *earn* this abundance at all. It's already yours. If, however, you believe you don't deserve it or are unworthy of it, you will block it with resistance (the very act of judging achieves this) and then the DWD will say, "See? You obviously don't deserve it, because if you did, you'd have it." It's quite diabolical. And he's got you right where he wants you.

Let go of the notions of "deserving" and "undeserving." They are serving only one entity, and keeping you out of Easy World, where everything is yours just for being there.

DWD LIE: There's a certain way things are supposed to be.

The DWD keeps you where he wants you by setting up expectations of how things are *supposed* to be, and then when they're different from that—as they pretty much always are—he feeds off your disappointment and anger. He keeps you so focused on one limited idea of how things are going to be that you miss the abundant gifts in how things really are!

When you choose Easy World instead of investing in how

Breathe...Relax...Allow...Enjoy

things are "supposed to be," you can relax and know that everything is unfolding according to the Design for Harmony to support your ultimate well-being. In Easy World, things may turn out differently than you expected, but you know they always turn out *better*! In Easy World, you are *always* rewarded, never punished.

> DWD LIE: If you don't have enough trouble, you need to borrow some.

Keeping your focus in the present moment aligns you with Easy World. Focusing anywhere else aligns you with Difficult World. So, you won't be surprised to learn that the Difficult World Dictator does his best to keep you focused anywhere *but* the present so that he can keep you in DW and devour all the energy you're shunting into it.

How does the DWD keep you out of the present moment? Sometimes it's through fixating on the past and fomenting regrets, but his chief strategy is *worry*. Worrying requires orienting yourself to the future and creating fearful scenarios to empower with your energy—just the kind of meal the DWD relishes.

The DWD is so devoted to your being in resistance, he *makes up* stuff for you to resist! I have always loved the expression "borrowing trouble" as a metaphor for worry. That's what worrying is. It's finding some trouble to put where there actually is none.

Remember the Law of Easy World? *Worry, strife, and struggle,*

Breathe...Relax...Allow...Enjoy

in any form, are strictly prohibited. You can't be in Easy World and worry.

Worry is a choice, not a requirement. When you realize that in Easy World, everything is working together to support your total well-being, and that worry is completely counterproductive—that it keeps you out of the realm of harmony and solutions—you'll opt out of worry and in to Easy World.

DWD LIE: Change is to be feared and avoided.

The DWD, with his devotion to resistance, promotes your attachment to having things stay the same forever. He wants you to believe that change is detrimental. But constant change is one of the primary characteristics of the universe in which we dwell. So right there, we have the makings of an ongoing challenge and an ongoing invitation to Difficult World. Change isn't detrimental—it's natural, and when you relax and stay in Easy World, it's always beneficial.

The more we resist the flow of energy and the transformation of forms, the more painful things are and the stronger Difficult World is in our experience. Resistance equals friction. If you've ever worn a new pair of shoes without socks and gotten a blister, you know that friction causes problems. Choosing Easy World, however, allows you to be fine with change and to flow with it, because in Easy World, you can see clearly that with every change your experience evolves to a higher level.

Breathe...Relax...Allow...Enjoy

DWD LIE: Doing something new is dangerous.

The DWD is absolutely anti-expansion. As the resistance master, he gets his kicks from saying no. Unless the DWD has planted an idea in your head because he knows it will lead to failure, and thus provide nutrients for him, he seems to relish giving you reasons why things aren't going to work in order to undermine your success.

He gets off on pointing out why what you are proposing can't happen, why it's a bad idea, and he thrives on keeping you from seeking solutions. He often throws in some impending doom if you don't turn back immediately.

Some of his favorite discouraging comments are: It's too risky. It will take too long. It's too much trouble. It can't be done. It's wrong. You can't afford it. You don't know what you're doing. That's crazy. And the DWD's favorite: It's too difficult. Of course, if you move ahead with your project anyway and it's a success, the DWD is first in line to claim credit for it!

When ego starts chiming in with its toxic, shut-down phrases, you have an antidote. Just say, "That's not true in Easy World, where everything is easy!" You can flip every one of those comments, and know that the opposite is true in the realm of all possibilities called Easy World.

"I can afford it *in Easy World.*" "It can be done *in Easy World.*" "It's easy *in Easy World.*" Ego specializes in creating its lies as exact opposites of the truth, so with this technique, you can actually use the fearful ego's downers as pep talks! And if the fearful ego is against something, you know it's probably a divine idea!

DWD LIE: Being better than someone else is vital.

Comparison is yet another invitation to Difficult World. It's a subtle thing—a slippery slope for sure. It's such a part of our culture and language, what could be the problem? Better, worse; more attractive, less attractive; richer, poorer; more intelligent, less intelligent; and so on, ad infinitum. Comparison is a judgment game, and judgment is the exclusive tool of the fearful ego.

You see, Creation is based on diversity. Comparisons, therefore, are ultimately meaningless. Every aspect of every being is unique and necessary in order to fulfill the Creator's desire to experience every possibility of existence. There is nothing in all of Creation that does not fulfill this desire; therefore, everything has its own singular value, despite how we judge it. We may try to make ourselves feel better by saying someone else is fatter or less intelligent, or has less wealth, but that only serves the DWD and keeps us out of Easy World.

I'm not going to suggest that you give up comparison completely, because having contrast—much of which is benign— makes our human existence interesting. It's the *intent* behind it. Simply be aware that when you are using comparison to feel superior or to put separation between yourself and someone or something else, you are under the jurisdiction of the DWD. And that means you're headed for pain.

Judgment and comparison as catalyzed by the fearful ego are fueled by fear—fear of not surviving. You see, status is key to survival in the gestalt of the one that runs the DWD's program. The higher the status in this entity's way of viewing things, the more likely one is to survive.

WHERE DOES ALL THAT FEAR COME FROM?

Why does the DWD do what he does? Your ego primarily runs off the impulses of the most primitive part of your brain; what is called in the triune brain theory the "R-complex," or your "reptilian brain." Reptilian . . . serpent . . . ring a bell? The reptilian-brain-driven ego is what was described as "the serpent" in the story of humanity's original exit from Easy World—it is the very entity that first seduced us out of it!

This is the selfsame entity that dictates your leaving Easy World every time it happens. The serpent in the story represents the reptilian brain that not only seduced Eve and Adam from the Garden, but that also is constantly inviting *you* out of Easy World, too.

Let me immediately reassure you that I am not putting down the reptilian brain or labeling it "evil." Heavens, no! Every human being has one, and there is a reason for that. It is a vital component if you want to be an embodied human being, since it is what keeps your heart beating, your lungs

Breathe . . . Relax . . . Allow . . . Enjoy

pumping—indeed, all your vital organs working—without your having to think about it. Your autonomic nervous system is controlled by this part of your brain.

It is also the mechanism that looks out for your physical survival in other ways. It is what causes adrenaline to dump into your system so you can jump out of the way of the bus that is about to run you over, what gives you the superhuman strength to lift a car off a loved one trapped beneath it or fight off an attacker. It is always on alert for anything that may threaten your survival or the survival of your tribe. Yes, it is first and foremost a physical-survival entity. At its foundation, however, you might say, is *fear*—fear of not surviving.

Your reptilian brain puts no stock whatsoever in your Spirit's ability to perceive the up-to-the-nanosecond workings of the Whole of Creation and guide you accordingly. Actually, more accurately, it doesn't even *know* about your Spirit. It doesn't have an awareness of the more evolved aspects of your brain that house your connection to your Spirit, or of the wisdom that channels through there. It is an important part of your Difficult World survival system, but it makes a lousy guide for living your life in harmony. It isn't designed for that purpose—your Spirit is.

See, when you are in Easy World, allowing your Spirit—your personal Easy World guide—to run your program, you won't be in the path of the bus to begin with. The Design for Harmony will not allow it. You'll never get run over by a bus in Easy World because such things don't—and can't—occur there! But your reptilian brain, which evolved separately and before the rest of

Breathe...Relax...Allow...Enjoy

your brain, is incapable of comprehending that, so it just keeps running its "You're always in danger" program.

If your reptilian brain had a motto, it might be "Something or someone is always out to get you." And because that's where your ego draws its input, that is one of ego's mottoes—and one of Difficult World's mottoes—too. You can easily see how this does not square up with the Design for Harmony!

If the Design for Harmony—Easy World—had a motto, it would be "Everyone and everything is always out to enhance your well-being." Quite a juxtaposition, isn't it? I'm sure you can see how listening to your fearful ego puts you in Difficult World and how listening to your Spirit puts you in Easy World.

THE ULTIMATE BUZZKILL

Your fearful ego is quite the smooth operator and can move in, grab the remote, and change the channel very rapidly—before you've even realized it's happened. Being able to recognize when this has occurred is important so you can choose Easy World before you get sucked into the depths of DW.

How many times have you been feeling empowered and hopeful, or had an exciting, expansive idea and been flying high and free like a helium balloon when, suddenly, it was as if someone yanked the string on your balloon and dragged you back to Earth? Or popped the balloon altogether? That was the Difficult World Dictator, putting you in your place—or, rather, *his* place.

Basically, your fearful ego is what is referred to in slang

Breathe...Relax...Allow...Enjoy

terms as a "buzzkill." Just get on a high—a natural high—the kind that comes from opening your heart and allowing Love to flow freely so that your vibrational frequency is elevated, the kind where you feel that anything is possible, where you're soaring with your Spirit, and your ego *flips out*. He moves in to shut you down as rapidly as possible, because that kind of expansiveness is threatening to his very existence.

Recently, I was flying high in the joy space. I had just finished my swim workout, which always raises my vibration, and I was counting my blessings and feeling a tremendous amount of appreciation and optimism. Suddenly, I felt my vibration drop with a jolt. It was like a gate suddenly closing on all the energy that had been coursing through me.

"You're a fool to let yourself feel this good. Something could happen to mess things up and then you'll feel really bad!"

It was only a split-second, nonarticulated thought until I slowed down and deciphered it. My fearful ego had stolen my joy by trying to scare me about the possibility of my joy being stolen!

Seriously. That DWD is one perverse—and effective—dude.

RECOGNIZING THE PRESENCE OF THE DWD

While there are those times, as in my story above, when you're immediately aware you've been hijacked by the Difficult World Dictator, it's not always that obvious. The DWD is so insidious, you may not even realize he's horned in and grabbed the remote until you're deep into playing the role he created for you on Channel 2 (in a melodrama, of course). But by paying attention to your thoughts and feelings and the sensations in your body, you can quickly choose Easy World before you sink too far into Difficult World.

Essentially, if your thoughts are at all fear-based, the DWD is behind them. If they are greedy, it's the DWD. If they are status-oriented, it's the DWD. If they are defensive or feature retaliation, it's the DWD. If they are critical, snarky, or otherwise judgmental, it's You Know Who. If what you're hearing/thinking is complicated or convoluted, it's the DWD. If the voice you're hearing is strident—well, I don't even need to tell you!

The actual vocabulary of the DWD is another indicator that he's the one who has commandeered the remote. Terms like "elite," "superior," "exclusive," "stupid," "against," "wrong"—terms that connote judging, resisting, dividing, or excluding—are sure tip-offs that your fearful ego is calling the shots and is drowning out the Love-filled voice of your Spirit.

Pay attention to your body's signals when you want to differentiate between the input you're receiving from your Spirit and the input you're receiving from your fearful ego. Your body doesn't lie, even when your ego does. It is designed to respond very definitely to varying levels of Love flowing—or not flowing. Though we've largely forgotten about this energy-monitoring tool, we can learn to rely on it again.

When ego is horning in, you can feel it shutting down the flow, damming up the energy, like the gates in a canal lock closing. Ego blocks the flow so that your vibration is lowered and

Breathe...Relax...Allow...Enjoy

you're in Difficult World. When this happens, you feel duller and less alive. Sometimes it makes you feel weary. It will *always* make you feel less joyful, of course.

There are times when your ego is on a roll because you're allowing "stuff" to flow—such as not-so-nice thoughts and feelings you've been resisting—and this release may cause you to feel very energized, but it's a temporary rush. Unless you are purposely doing this to "clear the pipe" so as to raise your vibration and get back to Easy World as I describe doing in Chapter 7, you will usually feel bad afterward.

Another common sign that your fearful ego is in the house is when your solar plexus is stirred up. That is your ego's favorite bodily hangout, and you may feel a knot in your stomach when ego has a stranglehold. (In the section called "Frequency-Raising Support Tools and Techniques" in Chapter 7, I give suggestions for remedying that. Look for "Soothing Your Solar Plexus.")

If you start paying attention, you'll soon be very aware of how your body responds to all kinds of influences and vibrational frequencies. I can't overemphasize the importance of this. Your body is designed to be a monitor of energy, and learning to read it is extremely empowering. Like an early warning system, before other, more unpleasant evidence shows up, it will tell you immediately when the DWD has moved in and you're not in Easy World anymore.

For more indicators that you're under the DWD's influence, you might want to refer back to Chapter 2 and the list of signs that you've left Easy World.

Breathe...Relax...Allow...Enjoy

THE DWD: MASTER VENTRILOQUIST

I'm sure you've experienced the voice of the DWD coming out of someone else's mouth. I know I have! Indeed, the DWD often speaks through others. It seems that all fearful egos are in league with one another, and support one another in keeping us in Difficult World.

If you are vulnerable to that, it's due to *your* fearful ego attracting a match for its own opinion. Fearful egos adore being channeled by other people, and they are absolutely empowered and emboldened by agreement and validation.

When you are truly ensconced in Easy World, the downer voices won't be audible because they're broadcasting on Channel 2, while you're tuned in to Channel 1. If you've got a foot in both worlds, however, then you are susceptible to their summons back to Difficult World, both from the DWD in your head and from your DWD appearing to speak through others. Use these invitations as cues for choosing Easy World!

OUR COLLECTIVE BELIEFS SUSTAIN DIFFICULT WORLD

The fearful ego has been lying to human beings forever, and over time he has not only managed to convince us that his lies are true, but he has also created a web of lies that are believed by most human beings to simply be *the way things are.* That's what Difficult World is: a web of lies. There is nothing authentic

Breathe...Relax...Allow...Enjoy

about it; it is entirely built on the illusions spun by this master fabricator that resides in us all.

So now there's a complex and enormous set of false belief systems that has been spun by the Difficult World Dictator and propagated at both the individual and the collective levels. We're born into this and programmed with it starting at the beginning of our lives, and unless we decide to choose Easy World, we largely abide by it till death, thus sustaining Difficult World for all, and of course, most acutely, for ourselves.

Pick just about any topic and you will find a whole system of DW beliefs around it. These are beliefs that have been put forth by the Difficult World Dictator and adopted by the entire culture, and thus they become true in Difficult World. Some general DW collective beliefs you may recognize are:

- Nothing worthwhile is ever easy.
- Life is hard, then you die.
- If something can go wrong, it will.
- If you meet an obstacle, push harder.
- No pain, no gain.
- You just have to suck it up and *make* yourself do certain things.
- Financial wealth is the key to security.
- The harder you work, the more successful you'll be.
- Nothing in life is free.

. . . and multitudes more. These beliefs are so entrenched in human consciousness, they've become clichés! I'm sure you can come up with a list of your own. Of course, none of these is actually true—at least, not in Easy World!

Since we create our experience according to our beliefs, the more we believe these DW notions, the more evidence we create to support our beliefs. The more evidence we see, the more we believe them based on the evidence we've created. And then there are all those other people agreeing that it's true—after all, just look at the evidence. What a system!

So, What's the Answer?

Well, it's for sure you can't out-resist the resistance master. When you go into any kind of resistance *about* the DWD or in response to him or anything else, you have moved into his clutches again. Therefore, fighting your fearful ego only makes things worse, because however frustrated or angry you are, you're simply feeding him a meal of the energy he prefers.

Remember, the Difficult World Dictator thrives on your frustration, revulsion, and anger. So, being *against* this entity with his potentially maddening dynamics is completely self-defeating and only strengthens him.

The way to deal successfully with the Difficult World Dictator is by choosing Easy World, of course! When you choose Easy World, you are not resisting what you *don't* want; you are embracing what you *do* want. Thus you are operating outside the territory of the fearful, resistant ego. Whenever you *accept,*

Breathe...Relax...Allow...Enjoy

embrace, or *allow,* instead of rejecting, blocking, or resisting, you automatically rise above the DWD.

Essentially, by choosing Easy World, you are choosing to allow Love/Life Force to flow freely in and through you without clamping down and resisting. Love is the key to being in Easy World. The fearful ego, however, is allergic to Love.

But when you decide you won't reduce the flow of Love through you for any reason, *not even to be irritated at the DWD,* you effectively neutralize the DWD, rising to the level where Difficult World is nonexistent and Easy World determines your experience.

I'd like to tell you that this will happen instantly, but you're going to need to be patient. (Impatience is the purview of the DWD, after all!) You've had a lifetime of erecting barriers to Love while answering the fearful ego's call to Difficult World, and it's an entrenched habit.

In time, though, after you've become more practiced at sustaining the flow, come what may, you will be able to stay on Channel 1 for longer and longer periods without interference. The more you're in Easy World, the more you'll have the power to *stay* in it. Meanwhile, you now have the tools to be aware of where you are in consciousness—of who has control of the clicker—and you can use them to remember to rechoose Easy World however many times it takes.

While right now it may seem that the Difficult World Dictator has the upper hand, he has only the amount of power we allow him to have. When you decide to be nonresistant—and I know

Breathe...Relax...Allow...Enjoy

this seems like a stretch—and actually *appreciate* the DWD's persistence, devotion to his cause, and ability to effectively do his job, it disempowers him.

I know, I know; usually, appreciating someone *em*powers him. But remember, the Difficult World Dictator's program is the opposite. Appreciation makes him disappear!

Appreciation, which is an extra-potent form of the resistance antidotes of accepting, embracing, and allowing, is an expressway to Easy World. So, instead of resisting the DWD and making him stronger, you can choose appreciation. When you notice him hanging around and doing his thing, you can say something like "Wow—you're amazingly tenacious!" or "You're doing a great job at keeping Difficult World going!"

If appreciating the DWD is too challenging, you can train yourself to simply appreciate something else whenever you notice that the DWD is active. It can be absolutely anything. As long as you're in the mode of appreciating and embracing *something,* you're out of resistance. I suggest training yourself to appreciate Easy World whenever you need to switch realities. I find that simply saying, "I love, love, *love* Easy World!" does the trick for me.

DEMOTE THE DWD

Here's some food for thought—some *empowering* food: What if we are the employers of the Difficult World Dictator? What if *we're* the ones who gave him his job to begin with? What if we,

Breathe...Relax...Allow...Enjoy

as curious, adventurous beings endowed with free will, who long ago decided we wanted to explore new realms beyond Easy World, needed the DWD to facilitate that?

What if the Difficult World Dictator did such an effective job that we descended so deeply into DW, we forgot how to get out? What if we even forgot there was anywhere else to be? What if we mistook the DWD's voice for the guidance system we were designed to follow? What if that was all a part of the plan to begin with, but we've forgotten it, being under the anesthesia of a lower vibrational frequency as we've been?

What if reading this book is your Spirit's way of reminding you of all that and of showing you how to override the DWD to find your way home to Easy World?

By choosing Easy World, we diminish the power of the Difficult World Dictator. By choosing Easy World *consistently,* we put him out of a job; indeed, we make him and Difficult World obsolete. And even if you're not to the point where you are able to or ready to be back in Easy World all the time, you can at least put him on part-time status so that you can spend more quality time at home in EW whenever you want to.

I choose to live in Easy World,

where everything is easy.

Breathe...Relax...Allow...Enjoy

6

Taking Action in Easy World

ction is quite an important facet of life in Easy World. Upon first hearing about Easy World, some people make the mistake of thinking that when you're there, you do absolutely nothing—that you just let the magical workings of the Universe and its agents do everything for you while you lie around eating bonbons. How much fun would *that* be? Okay . . . how much fun would that be after a couple of days?

While there is plenty of opportunity to be completely relaxed without needing to do anything in particular toward manifesting your intentions while things work out on your behalf as if by magic, Easy World is not a passive place. No, not at all. Easy World is a reality where your participation is vital.

We're human beings, with the propensity and desire for action, as well as passion for particular activities that bring us great joy. Our bodies, which are kinetic masterpieces, were made to be instruments of action. So, *of course* Easy World includes taking action. But not just any action, and not at just any time. It must be in alignment with the Design for Harmony, and it must be taken at just the right moment.

When what you do is in alignment with the Design for Harmony, it's always struggle-free, often deeply satisfying, and frequently fun. And, of course, it's easy! Easy World action is never difficult or disagreeable. While it will certainly sometimes be challenging—in a satisfying way—it always feels right and harmonious. If it doesn't, you're just not in Easy World and need to get on back there!

In Easy World, you simply stay relaxed, doing whatever is pleasurable to you and brings you joy (pleasure and joy are signs of being in alignment). And while what you feel like doing may often be the equivalent of lying around eating bonbons, such as taking a nap, reading a book, playing a game, or puttering in the garden—activities that all have great value in Easy World—there will be other times when you'll be much more active, depending on what you feel like doing. There will definitely be times, too, when you will experience the urge to take focused, dynamic, situation-specific action.

If there is something in particular you need to do to facilitate the manifestation of a desire, the harmonious outworking of a problem you've created in Difficult World, or some other matter, you will *feel* like taking action and innately know what to do. There's no forcing yourself to act in Easy World. If you

Breathe...Relax...Allow...Enjoy

have to *make* yourself do something, you know you've slipped back into Difficult World.

For your action to be in alignment with the Design for Harmony it must conform with Easy World's very simple guidelines governing action, which are *quite* different from those of Difficult World. When these conditions for harmonious action are met, what you experience is unqualified success and an increase in joy and fulfillment. Such action is easy, efficient, and effective; it is never laborious or strenuous, and certainly never in vain, the way Difficult World actions so often are.

What must you do to ensure that you are in alignment with Easy World when you act? The only kind of action that works in Easy World is inspired, energized action. Therefore, the Easy World ordinance for action is this: *Act only when inspired and energized.*

AN URGE

Let's examine those words "inspired" and "energized." *Inspired* means that your Spirit is motivating you from within. Your Spirit, in continuous, perfect alignment with Source and the Design for Harmony, always knows exactly what needs to be done. It is aware not only of what you need to do, but also of precisely the right time for your action to bear fruit and for you to hop to it. Then, and only then, it gives you the sign to act.

Rarely, if ever, will your Spirit tell you in advance what your appropriate action will be and when to take it, nor will you be given energy for a task in advance of the inspiration. You will know what action you are to take at exactly the right time, and you will receive the energy then, too.

Your Spirit provides the information and energy on a need-to-know basis because it is constantly attuned with and monitoring the Whole of Creation, a continuously shifting entity. Coordinating with it requires the precision of being fully in the present moment. You may get hints of what you will be doing in the future, but don't bank on those hunches, since they are likely ego's guesses. And what seems to need to be done at one point may not be at all what is required when it is, indeed, time for you to act.

How does your Spirit inspire you? It informs you through an urge or a thought that may come in the form of a sudden realization or "lightbulb moment," a gentle knowing, or even an unconscious prompting as to what you need to do in order to facilitate the perfect, harmonious resolution of things. It gives you the signal to do your part when conditions are exactly right to do it.

Of course, you must be available to *receive* these signals from your Spirit. If you are engaged in worry, in trying to figure things out, or in trying to *make* things happen, you are definitely out of Easy World, and most likely will not be aware when your Spirit is giving you the alert to take the ideal action that will move things efficiently and effectively along to harmonious resolution.

Not only that, if you take action while you're in Difficult

Breathe...Relax...Allow...Enjoy

World, and base it on your fearful ego's promptings instead of your Spirit's, you might very well be acting contrary to your—and others'—highest interests. To receive inspiration for taking the action needed to facilitate your well-being, and the well-being of all, *you need to be sufficiently relaxed and open to it.*

Isn't it a relief to know that being relaxed and doing what feels joyful to you is not the guilty pleasure you may have thought it was, but the very requirement to ensure that things are facilitated successfully?

A SURGE

Along with the inspiration, you will feel *energized* to do whatever is required of you. *Energized* means that the energy has arisen within you to do what needs doing. When you receive your Spirit's prompting to do what you are to do, you will feel energy welling up in you to do it. In other words, along with the *urge*, you will feel a *surge*—a surge of energy.

If it's time to act, it won't be a case of having an idea but being too tired to do anything about it. If you're too tired or just don't feel like doing something, that means it's not time for you to do whatever it is you think you need to do! When the time is right, and you're in Easy World, you'll have both the inspiration and the irrepressible energy to follow through. You can depend on it. Even if it's something you haven't really been keen to do, the energy will sweep you through it and you'll get it done with ease.

Breathe . . . Relax . . . Allow . . . Enjoy

Sometimes, when energy arises in you in response to an inspiration, it will be a subtle thing. It may happen that before you even realize what you're doing, you will automatically find you're taking the appropriate action. Other times, it will bubble up so strongly that you'll feel you are unable to sit still any longer—that you simply *must* act or you'll explode! When this occurs, it is highly inadvisable to resist it. And yes, resisting the energy of an inspiration will send you right out of Easy World, just as doing the opposite—acting without inspiration and the accompanying energy—will.

The energy to act will always be commensurate with what needs to be done. Energy will always accompany inspiration, even if it is, for example, just enough to make a phone call. Sometimes, that's all the action required on your part. If that's what you're inspired to do, and that's the level of energy you're experiencing, you can trust that, for now, that's all that's required. Trying to do more before more energy shows up will take you out of EW.

You'll discover that one of ego's favorite tricks to pull you back into Difficult World is to tell you that you're being lazy when you do only what matches your energy to act. Don't buy it. When you relax and know that you're always provided with the exact right amount of energy for you to do your part at any given time, you will experience the magic of Easy World and see that all gets done effectively, with efficiency, and in perfect time.

Breathe...Relax...Allow...Enjoy

Just trust that if major energy is required, major energy will be supplied. You will never be called upon to do anything in Easy World that isn't funded with energy. The same cannot be said for Difficult World, as I'm sure you've experienced.

NO INSPIRATION OR ENERGY? THEN IT'S ONE OF THESE THREE THINGS

If you perceive that something needs doing, and you've chosen Easy World but are not inspired and energized to take action, then you can trust that one of three things is true:

1. It isn't yet time to do it (and the inspiration and energy will be showing up as an indicator of when it *is* time).
2. It's someone else's task to accomplish, and you need to relax and allow whoever *is* inspired and energized to handle what needs to be done. (I call other human beings who facilitate things in Easy World "Easy World agents.")
3. Despite how it may seem, it actually doesn't need doing at all. (You'll often be shown why later.)

My favorite story that illustrates number 2 is quite mundane and personal. One morning as I finished breakfast, I realized that I had eaten the last of our supply of fresh fruit. I had really been enjoying eating berries for breakfast, and I was disappointed to think of not having any for the next day.

Breathe...Relax...Allow...Enjoy

My ego-mind suggested I drag myself out to the store and get some fruit to make sure I didn't have to go without, but I was absorbed in a writing project, and even though I definitely wanted more fruit, I simply did not feel inspired or energized to go to the store and get any. So I shrugged my shoulders and thought, "Well, I'll get some fruit somehow." My doubtful self chimed in with "And if I don't, it won't kill me to go without." I sighed, invoked Easy World again, then went back to my writing and forgot all about it.

When Rick arrived home from work that afternoon, he called out, "Sweetie! I brought home a surprise for you!" Excited by his tone and by the prospect of a surprise, I hustled to meet him to see what it could be. To my utter delight, it was several cartons of fresh raspberries and blueberries!

Now, it's useful to know that I had not mentioned the fruit, or a lack thereof, to him at all. Indeed, I had totally let the matter go, and may not even have thought of it again till breakfast the next morning. When I asked him what had possessed him to get the berries, he said, "I just knew how much you've been loving having fruit for breakfast, and I knew berries were on sale, so I decided to stop at the store on the way home to get you some."

Perfect! I was in Easy World. I had a desire. I trusted that somehow it would be provided for. I did not force myself to disrupt my writing to go to the store when I felt no inspiration or energy to; instead I dropped all concern for my needs (basically, I got out of the way), and Easy World came through, as it always does.

Breathe...Relax...Allow...Enjoy

And it was not just a benefit to me. Rick, who was tuned in to his own inspiration and energy, was gratified to be aligned with the Design for Harmony, acting on the idea and the energy that was communicated to him via his own Spirit. He, acting as an Easy World Agent, following his own inspiration and energy to act, enhanced both his experience and mine. I felt happy; he felt happy. Easy World is definitely the realm of win-win.

EVERYTHING THAT NEEDS TO GET DONE ALWAYS DOES IN EASY WORLD

We may worry that if we stop pushing and relax, we'll forget or neglect to do whatever it is we believe needs doing, and then our little universe will collapse. After all, there's *so* much to do! We are told by our fearful egos that there is not enough time or resources to get done all there is to do, and that puts us in a tizzy (*tizzy* being the scientific term for the state you achieve when you are sufficiently sucked into Difficult World's swirling vortex). This, of course, ensures we're in too much turmoil to be productive.

The idea that there's too much to do and too little time and energy in which to get it done is just not true, despite how real it seems. It's (surprise, surprise!) another one of ego's traps to pull us into Difficult World. The fearful ego is quite the expert at creating scary holograms to intimidate you into freaking out.

The Difficult World Dictator knows that the stress of feeling

Breathe...Relax...Allow...Enjoy

overwhelmed and pressured and facing what seem to be impossible odds, with a little impending doom thrown in for good measure, will put you just where he wants you every time . . . unless you know to choose Easy World. Easy World is the antidote to feeling overwhelmed.

There's always time for everything that authentically needs to be done in Easy World. When necessary, time even stretches in this amazing realm that does not conform to the same physical laws as Difficult World! Time is elastic in Easy World and can expand and contract according to need. Remember my story about our EW trip to Lake Michigan from Chapter 3—the one where we got to our destination in an amount of time that was impossible if calculated by ordinary means? The physical restraints of time and space in Difficult World are not necessarily factors in Easy World.

When you're in Easy World, everything that needs doing is done in perfect time and efficiency while you stay relaxed, confident, and joyful. And so often what our ego-minds have told us just *has* to be done, really doesn't. Things that don't actually need doing now either get postponed till it's the right time to deal with them, or they evaporate.

And, as in my berry surprise story, anything that needs to be done now that you're not inspired and energized to handle yourself gets done by Easy World's Agents as if by magic.

Breathe . . . Relax . . . Allow . . . Enjoy

SHOULDS: SO VERY DIFFICULT WORLD

It is vital that we learn to tell the difference between a prompting from our Spirits and one coming from the fearful ego—our own, or those of others. Any call to action not coming through your Spirit as inspiration can probably be labeled as a should, an ought-to, a supposed-to, or a have-to. These feel like pressure and usually lead to resistance and discomfort.

Shoulds and have-tos, of course, are just ego devices for calling you out of Easy World. When you respond to these DW–based motivators that are originating either with your own fearful ego or the ego of someone else influential in your life, you will find yourself smack-dab in the center of Difficult World, feeling resentful. Resentment is definitely a DW anchor.

Why would we let the ego-based demands of others mandate what we do? Because we fear that if we don't dance to their tune, we'll somehow be less loved, we'll lose status, or something else undesirable will happen. Guess what? That's another trick of the DWD to keep you in Difficult World. (Anytime fear is involved, you know who's behind it!) You may certainly create it to go down that way—the way that you're fearing—but you don't have to.

When you honor your own feelings and say no to doing things that someone else wants you to do but that you're truly not inspired and energized to, you are doing both of you a favor. You are honoring the Design for Harmony and offering the other person an invitation to join you there. They may not

Breathe...Relax...Allow...Enjoy

fully appreciate it in the moment, but, like my friend did after I declined her invitation to dinner years ago, they may later.

I had been to her home for dinner a few nights before, and when she asked me again, I felt no inspiration or energy to go. She was newly separated from her husband and I knew she was lonely. As her friend, I would have gone, of course, if I had felt the slightest inspiration to, but when she invited me, I strongly intuited that it was not the thing to do. I could sense that it was her fearful ego issuing the invitation to try to avoid being alone with herself, facing the inevitable.

I briefly contemplated whether I *should* go, but the answer was clearly "No." When I said, kindly but without an excuse, that coming over was not what I needed to do that night, she asked me if I already had plans. When I said that I didn't, and offered no reason for not going other than that it didn't feel like the right thing for me to do, the silence was palpable, but she let it go without further protest.

It was only many years later—long after it had slipped my mind—that she mentioned it again, and when she did, it was to thank me.

"When you did that, I was hurt," she admitted, "but I know you did the right thing. I was really able to get in touch with my feelings of abandonment that night when I was alone so that I could start to heal them. And the way you handled it taught me a valuable lesson about being true to myself. Because *you* were true to *yourself* and said no to me when that was what felt right to you, and you did it without flinching or making up an

Breathe...Relax...Allow...Enjoy

excuse, I learned what being true to oneself looks like. Now I do that for me. I am truly grateful for that experience. It liberated me!"

One of the most empowering things you can do for yourself and others is to be true to your own relationship with the Design for Harmony and do only what you are inspired to do. Pay attention to your motivation for action, and if there is a "should" behind it, consider whether or not it is going to enhance your life to follow through on it. (A hint: Operating outside the Design for Harmony never will.) If not, be sure you're in Easy World, centered in Love, and as clearly, kindly, and gracefully as possible, opt out.

You can trust that if doing something isn't right for you, it won't be right for anyone else, either. The only Easy World reason for action is *inspiration*. If you do anything for any other reason, you are not in Easy World, and you are not in alignment with the Design for Harmony; therefore, nobody wins.

Though shoulds are usually provided by other people, they can also be your own mental constructs based on conclusions you've drawn from the world around you. They may be rules you picked up from your parents, teachers, or other role models. Consider the grim humor in this: You may still be allowing your actions to be dictated by the egos of people who have been out of your life for decades, and some of them may not even be on the planet anymore!

Just say yes to Easy World, and you automatically say no to shoulds.

Breathe...Relax...Allow...Enjoy

Procrastination Is Nonexistent in Easy World

An adjunct to the "should" mechanism is "procrastination." Procrastination is one of the Difficult World Dictator's many methods to sabotage you. In Easy World, there's no procrastination, because there's no arbitrary pressure to do anything. There's nothing to push against. You are either naturally inspired and energized and eager to do something, or you do nothing.

Procrastination happens when you are trying to retain or regain your own energy autonomy by resisting. It happens when you are resisting having to do something without being inspired and energized to do it. Of course, waiting for inspiration and energy is purely Easy World, but when resistance enters the picture, you're in Difficult World.

You can't be in Easy World, attuned with the Design for Harmony and your Spirit's guidance, when you're busy rebelling against whomever the should is coming from, be it your mother, your spouse, or the DWD in your own mind. You need to drop the resistance in order to transcend procrastination.

All you need to do is to simply invoke Easy World, breathe, relax, allow, and enjoy, and trust that you will be inspired and energized to do what needs doing when the timing is right, no matter what anyone, including your ego, says. If you're a self-professed procrastinator, you may be amazed at all the energy

Breathe...Relax...Allow...Enjoy

you free up and how productive you become just by releasing resistance and simply moving into alignment with Easy World's guidelines about action!

Despite what your fearful ego may tell you, sometimes the appropriate action *is* no action at all—what some might incorrectly label procrastination. Sometimes there is an important reason behind postponing something that *seems* to need to be done sooner rather than later, as was reinforced for me in the following domestic episode.

There was a large pot of flowers on our front porch as there is each summer, and I hadn't watered the flowers in quite a while. I knew they must be very thirsty, but I kept not watering them. Either I'd forget them till I was on my way somewhere in a hurry and not have time to stop when I spotted them, or I was on my way back, my arms laden with stuff, when I noticed them, but then forgot them.

Or—and this was the odd part—I'd think about watering them and nix the idea for no particular reason that I could think of other than I just didn't feel like doing it, all the while wondering why in the world I was waiting when it obviously needed to be done, and when doing it would require so little. And the pot got drier and drier as I seemed almost unable to take action.

The flowers didn't seem to be suffering yet, but I knew it would be a stress on them if I didn't quench their thirst pretty soon. I caught myself fretting over what was, in reality, a pretty innocuous thing, so I decided to relax about it in true

Breathe...Relax...Allow...Enjoy

EW style, and trust that I'd be prompted to water them when the time was right. I hoped I'd be able to understand the oddity of this strange paralysis of will at some point, and sure enough, I soon was.

Late in the afternoon, as I peered out the window to look at the deluge that had started outside, I could see that the pot, back a ways from the overhang that protects the porch from the weather, wasn't getting any of the water that was pouring from the sky in a great torrent. At that moment I felt an urge and a surge, and immediately, I went to get the watering can because, at last, the inspiration and the energy to water those flowers had shown up.

As I stood on the covered front porch in the rainstorm, surveying the scene after giving the flowers a drink, I noticed that water was gushing from the gutter because one of the front downspouts had detached itself. The water was no longer being diverted out into the yard, but was pouring right onto the ground next to the basement window well!

We'd had basement flooding before caused by just such a thing, which is why we'd had new gutters and downspouts installed. Believing the problem was solved, we would never have thought to check the downspouts. Fortunately, Rick was able to quickly reattach the long pipe that had come loose, thereby averting a flooding disaster.

If I had watered the flowers anytime in the couple of days since I first thought to do it, I probably wouldn't have been out

Breathe...Relax...Allow...Enjoy

there during the downpour, and the front porch is the only vantage point from which that particular downspout can be seen without going out in the yard, which we weren't likely to do in a storm. How grateful I am that I did not force myself to water the flowers and, instead, followed the Easy World guidelines for action!

Once you let go of the notion of procrastination—once you stop rebelling against the external (and internal) voices trying to get you to act on a schedule other than your Spirit's—you free yourself up to receive true inspiration accompanied by the motivation and energy to act on things right away if that's what is called for.

AND YET ANOTHER FEARFUL EGO TRICK

Not only will the DWD try to make you do things at times that don't fit with the Design for Harmony, or do things that do not actually need to be done, he will often pooh-pooh the promptings to action coming to you from your Spirit. If they seem not to fit the ego's perception of what needs to occur, or (and this is a biggie) if the instruction seems illogical, the ego will tell you, often derisively, that what your Spirit is guiding you to do is nonsensical and to ignore it. Don't.

Know, of course, that though you may not fully understand why you're being inspired to do something—or *not* do something—and it may not make logical sense to you, your

Breathe...Relax...Allow...Enjoy

Spirit's guidance will never tell you to do something harmful. If you feel that what you're being prompted to do is something like that, it is *not* your Spirit, and you need to simply invoke Easy World again and stay tuned for true inspiration.

While you may sometimes be guided to do something that someone else's ego will choose to be in a snit about, never will you be inspired to do actual harm. Most often, what you are guided to do in Easy World ultimately enhances everyone's feelings of wholeness, happiness, and fulfillment. And always, it will contribute to greater well-being for all.

A GREAT BONUS: BEING AN EASY WORLD AGENT

Yes, taking action is an intrinsic part of life in Easy World, and not just so your own specific needs, desires, and intentions are fulfilled, but so that you are an *agent* of Easy World, prospering the Whole. Every single thing that occurs in Easy World affects every part of Creation in a beneficial way.

Even when what you're doing seems purely selfish, it always benefits everyone and everything, as well as yourself, as long as you are in alignment with the Design for Harmony through following Easy World's action principles. Whatever you do in Easy World contributes to the great dance of evolution that is always occurring there.

Though you will rarely be able to see just how something you do in Easy World—perhaps even something very small and

Breathe...Relax...Allow...Enjoy

seemingly insignificant—makes a profound difference and creates greater well-being for all, be assured that it truly does.
When you are in Easy World, not only is everything working
together to support your own well-being, but everything *you*
do is an integral part of its magic. Isn't that cool?

I choose to live in Easy World,

where everything is easy.

Breathe...Relax...Allow...Enjoy

7

Finding Easy World
in the Dark

There will likely be at least a few occasions when moving into Easy World the usual way is not working. While there may be times when you won't be able to pinpoint why that's happening, it usually occurs when we have become embroiled in what we call "problems." In Difficult World, you are bound to encounter situations that range from merely vexing to downright devastating.

As long as we're living at least part-time in Difficult World (and who isn't at this point?), problems are a given because Difficult World is the very *world* of problems! In DW, you are vulnerable to turmoil, conflict, fragmentation, and devitalization, and the effects are not pretty—to anyone but the Difficult World Dictator, that is.

The Difficult World Dictator *needs* problems to keep you

tied up in Difficult World; problems keep Difficult World turning and the DWD fed. Thus, the Difficult World Dictator
works overtime to be sure that he turns every situation he possibly can into a problem by getting you to join him in his favorite activity: *resisting*. At these times, the DWD is really digging
in his heels to keep you from relaxing and allowing, the key
actions necessary for entering Easy World.

It's the Resistance—Always, the Resistance

Like Chinese handcuffs—those little woven straw tubes you
insert your index fingers into that tighten up, pinch, and trap
you as you try to pull your fingers back out—Difficult World
tightens around you when you resist a situation. It's a trap. The
more resistance you apply, the harder and more painful things
get, the more you don't like them, the worse you feel, the deeper
you sink into DW, and the darker things are, and so on.

　　While it is completely understandable for you to be deeply
upset and to try to resist what is happening when certain things
occur—things we consider to be serious problems, such as losing your job, losing your home, being behind in paying your
bills, life-threatening illness, divorce, or the death of a loved
one—it doesn't negate the truth that it's your *resistance* that
makes it hurt. Remember, resistance creates friction, and friction is what causes pain. And the longer you resist, the longer
the pain lasts.

Breathe...Relax...Allow...Enjoy

You can't escape until you relax and stop resisting. And the antidote to resisting is embracing, accepting, and allowing. But how in the world do you do that when you so desperately want something *not* to be happening and the Difficult World Dictator is continually turning your attention to the painful, fearful aspects of it all? How do you do this when the DWD has a vise grip on you and won't willingly let you leave Difficult World?

You have to *tranquilize* him so you can move into Easy World through the back door. You need to do those things that disempower him so that he is unable to resist. Just as putting an alligator on its back and rubbing its belly with sand puts it to sleep, certain activities you engage in will lull the DWD into submission. When that happens, you rise back up to Easy World.

When you're having trouble getting to Easy World for any reason, you just need to anesthetize the DWD and take the alternate route home.

What Is This Alternate Route?

Even before you discovered Easy World and knew you could deliberately choose to be in it, you had experiences in Easy World. Not just long ago and far away, but from time to time throughout your lifetime, as interludes in your Difficult World existence, you found yourself in Easy World.

Perhaps it was when you were newly in love with someone, or when you gazed upon your newborn for the first time, romped with your puppy, watched the sun set over the ocean, sat in your

Breathe...Relax...Allow...Enjoy

garden and appreciated its beauty, danced till you couldn't dance any more, had a gigglefest with your best friend, or got caught up in the music at a concert. That's because at those times, your vibration was spontaneously higher.

Your mind, embracing the experience and overwhelmed by Love, simply dropped resistance and allowed energy to flow freely, thus raising your vibration to the level of Easy World. So, the other approach to moving into Easy World is to take specific steps to raise your vibrational level; steps that automatically anesthetize and bypass your fearful ego. Problems are created in lower-vibration Difficult World, and solved in higher-vibration Easy World.

Though I can't say with any authority that Albert Einstein was aware he was describing the problem-solving power of moving to a higher vibration, the celebrated genius spoke to this phenomenon in one of his most famous quotes: "The significant problems we face cannot be solved at the same level of thinking we were at when we created them."

How you perceive a problem—or set of problems—is completely dependent on where you are on the vibrational scale. The lower you are, the darker and more hopeless things look, and the more muddled your thinking. The higher you go, the brighter things are, the more hopeful things look, the clearer your thinking, and the more obvious the solution becomes. And the more joyful you are.

While it's true that vibrational elevation frequently happens spontaneously, you don't have to wait till the stars align and

Breathe...Relax...Allow...Enjoy

everything falls into place for the DWD to drop resistance. You can assist it in happening. You can engage in activities that transcend the fearful ego to intentionally raise your vibration and move into the joy, ease, peace, and higher wisdom of Easy World through the back door.

In this chapter, I'm going to share my tried-and-true favorites with you. I'm betting that many of these are things you already just naturally do to lift yourself up when you're feeling low and out of the flow, but you may never have looked at them as techniques for raising your vibration or moving back into Easy World.

I find it profoundly empowering to have a designated system in place for doing this so that when you're feeling stuck, you know where to turn and what to do. It's for sure the Difficult World Dictator is not going to help you remember it when you're in the midst of something!

Before I give you the system, I'd like to tell you how I discovered it.

THE ANSWER TO A PRAYER

A quick review: Our emotions are tied to our vibrational frequency, as are our perceptions, our level of consciousness, and all aspects of our experience. The higher your vibration, the more joyful you are; the lower your vibration, the less joyful. When you raise your vibration, your emotional response is joy.

When you drop to a lower vibration, your emotional re-

Breathe...Relax...Allow...Enjoy

sponse to that is less than joy—sometimes, *way* less than joy—
and when your vibration is low enough, the response is depression.
My own forays into depression and my craving for greater happiness is how I was blessed with the Step-by-Step Frequency-
Raising System.

It was given to me as the answer to a prayer—many prayers,
actually. I spent most of my life being a victim of my emotions,
and I was in pain a lot, in a low-grade depression with a pasted-on
smiley face. But I also frequently experienced emotional highs
of connection and joy. Those, of course, were the times I liked!
Though I was never diagnosed with bipolar disorder, I'm guess-
ing I would have been if I had sought medical help for it.

One day, when I was particularly down and, for the gazil-
lionth time, feeling a sort of paralysis of will—an inability to
do anything, or even to remember the ideas I'd been so passionate about not long before—I cried out to Spirit, "This is
crazy! I don't want to do this anymore. *Please help me find a way
to just be happy!*"

While it hardly *seemed* like the thing that would lead to joy,
just after I said this, I felt like dissolving in self-pity. I had learned
to trust that what I felt like doing in response to a prayer, whether
it made sense to me or not, was probably the thing that was in
alignment at that time. So I threw myself something of a pity
party.

I found myself inspired to put on a CD by one of my favorite
singer-songwriters, who composed and recorded it while using
her musical creativity to move herself forward out of a major

Breathe...Relax...Allow...Enjoy

personal trauma. I had discovered, back when my canine side-kick had died a couple of years earlier, that listening to it helped me grieve. Now, as I listened to the woman sing of trying to survive, and express her feelings of betrayal, loss, and grief, emotions welled up, and the floodgates opened.

I got in touch with a sadness and an anger so deep within me that at first, it felt as if it might kill me if I allowed it to express itself, but Spirit nudged me to let it out, and so I did. I cried and wailed and, at times, when rage came to the surface, I expressed it as well. It was almost like watching a character in a movie, so detached was I from what was going on—and still, I managed to get into it.

I knew what was coming out of me was not really my core truth, or even what I actually believed about things. But some contrary, ignoble, not-very-loving, and, frankly, potty-mouthed part of me—the entity I'd now call the Difficult World Dictator—seemed to need to speak its piece, so I let it, even though it wasn't pretty.

No. Not pretty. But it was certainly effective.

As I allowed all the emotional energy to emerge and move out, I realized what a lot I had been stuffing down and holding back from my consciousness. It seemed that, nice girl that I was, I'd been using the aforementioned smiley face to tape shut a bottomless repository of not-very-nice thoughts and feelings. After forty or so minutes of off-and-on crying and yelling, I realized I was feeling much clearer and very calm.

I had some of my essential oils at hand, and felt drawn to the

Breathe...Relax...Allow...Enjoy

blend called "Release." Seconds after I inhaled its aroma, all residual sadness, depression, and angst just evaporated. As the CD was ending, I noticed that the song was one of triumph over trauma, and I was feeling the same!

The next CD that happened to be in the queue was an upbeat instrumental favorite of mine, something I would not have felt like listening to before my emotional release session. It was a little too peppy and light for my mood then, but now it was perfect. I listened to it while I made some notes about the experience, and generally just basked in the peaceful, happy feeling.

Another CD started, and it happened to be my favorite full-out joy music. I found myself dancing and singing with my heart leaping up in joy and celebration! I could feel the Love welling up and radiating from me powerfully. All kinds of creative ideas were coming into my mind and I was challenged to write them all down while still moving to the beat!

So, how in the world did I go from too depressed to do anything or even think clearly to a state of joy, energy, and creative thinking in such a short time? Without knowing what to call it, I had applied what I would later come to name the Step-by-Step Frequency-Raising System, the answer to my prayer!

The next time I was feeling down, I got out my notes and deliberately did pretty much exactly what I had done that first time. Lo and behold, it worked just as well! I had less sadness and anger to let out, but I released what was there, and I moved out of depression and into the clear space of spiritual connectedness and joy—Easy World—again.

Breathe...Relax...Allow...Enjoy

What I was given to understand by my Spirit is that the "pity party," the allowing of the fearful ego to express himself, is critical to the healing process. The DWD needs to be *heard* and his opinions (albeit based in lies) allowed to be expressed before he will pick his foot up off the garden hose and allow Love to flow freely again.

When you deny him the right to vent and, instead, stuff down the fear and other emotions that have arisen in response to listening to the DWD and being in Difficult World, you are in resistance—major resistance. So, like it or not, and though you probably stuffed down that misaligned energy to start with because it didn't feel good, getting it moving through you and out of you is really, really important.

Please recognize that when I recommend letting your fearful ego express himself, and allowing the feelings you've repressed to flow, I don't mean that you are letting your fearful ego take over. Not at all. What you're doing is purposefully *allowing* him to express what he needs to so the resistant energy dissipates. When you're the one consciously doing the allowing, it means that you're the one who is in charge.

You stay in the observer and "allower" role. You are being a manager here—managing your vibration through managing your feelings (and vice versa). Like I found myself spontaneously doing, you allow the energy to move while observing it as if you are watching an actor in a play do a really amazing, Academy Award–winning job of being emotional. It's not that you don't feel your feelings, it's that you don't *dissolve* into them. You are the coach that encourages the expression of them at the same time you're expressing them.

I continued to put the system to the test and began to be inspired to try out additional tools to move even higher on the scale. As I did this on a regular basis, my periods of depression were fewer and fewer, and my vibrational state held at a consistently higher level. By using this system, I raised my vibrational set point (my average vibrational level). I was, indeed, happier in general, just as I had prayed to be. As long as I practiced what I now call "vibrational management," I was a happy camper. And I still am as long as I don't neglect my emotional housecleaning!

Because I didn't always have an hour or more to apply the Step-by-Step System, I experimented and found that because I had cleared out much of the ancient repository of stagnant emotional energy I had been stuffing down, I could move from a low-energy state to a high-vibe state in a very short amount of time. Just like a maintenance housecleaning is faster once you've done a full spring cleaning, this process is faster once you've cleared out the long-stored blockages.

By simply abbreviating the steps—still going through them all, but just doing it faster—and utilizing some of the many simple but powerful tools I'm going to share with you to move yourself higher without putting the fearful ego into resistance, you, too, will find that you can move into the joy space almost instantly in many cases. (Of course, if you go ahead and express

Breathe...Relax...Allow...Enjoy

any emotion as it arises instead of stuffing it down, that will go a long way toward keeping your vibration up!) At first, though, take your time.

So, without further ado, here is a concise guide to approaching Easy World by the alternate route. Use this method anytime you need to escape the Difficult World Dictator, whether you're just a little down or you're in the midst of a full-blown problem.

THE STEP-BY-STEP FREQUENCY-RAISING SYSTEM

Step One: **Observe your feelings** and listen to the conversation in your head without judging what you observe. Pay attention to your solar plexus to see if it's clear or congested. If you feel angry, resentful, hurt, sad, fearful, or anything other than joyful; if your stomach is in a knot; or if what you're hearing in your head is other than loving, your fearful ego, the Difficult World Dictator, has taken the wheel.

He is depressing your vibrational frequency and keeping you out of Easy World by blocking the flow of Love through you. He has you in the "misery matrix," also known as Difficult World. Recognizing this is a very important first step.

Step Two: **State your intention** to move back to the higher-vibrational space of Easy World. Your intention brings all your energy to focus and informs your left brain that there is about

Breathe...Relax...Allow...Enjoy

to be a shift. Declare your desire to realign with your Spirit, and thus with the Source of Love/Life Force.

Being aligned with Source is necessary for Love to flow. Express your willingness to allow Love to flow freely again. If you don't feel willing, saying "I'm *willing* to be willing to allow Love to flow freely again" will usually do the trick. Surrender the process to your Spirit and know that you will be guided and enfolded every step of the way.

Step Three: **Allow your ego to express whatever it needs to**, whether it's rage, grief, or self-righteousness. Just let it come out. Cry, yell, punch a pillow—do whatever you need to do to discharge the energy. Encourage the release of this energy and do not resist anything that comes up on the basis of its not being "nice." If it helps, ask yourself who and what you're mad at or sad about, and see what comes tumbling out.

Playing sad or angry music can be very helpful in facilitating this. Prime the pump however you can (without harming yourself or anyone else, of course). The point is to get it all out of your system. If writing out your feelings (for your eyes only) would be helpful, do that. Though you may find your ego needs to vent about a perceived insult or injury from someone else, these exercises are *for you and no one else*—ideally, you will do them in private.

Observe without resistance while this emotional purging is going on, and know that these feelings are not an intrinsic part of you, but simply "stuff" that needs to be discharged to make

Breathe...Relax...Allow...Enjoy

way for Love to flow and your vibrational frequency to rise so you can move back into Easy World and joy. (If you feel hesitant about discharging emotional pollution into the environment, simply state at the outset that once released, it will return to being pure Love again.)

Devote as much purposeful time to this as needed. Step Three is *not optional* if you want results!

Step Four: **Utilize any frequency-raising support activities and tools that seem appropriate** as soon as you've vented and are feeling clearer. (See the list in the next section.) Your Spirit will inspire you to select the ones that will be most effective, in the most effective order. Allow yourself to simply gravitate to the ones you are attracted to. Attraction is an indicator that they will bring you into closer alignment with the Design for Harmony.

Step Five: **Give in to the upward movement of your energy** and enhance it by breathing into it and celebrating it! Your breath will always take you higher. Stay focused on the wonderful feeling of Life Force flowing through you, and feel it elevating you closer and closer to the "joy space." Feel the powerful magnetic energy of Easy World calling you upward, and revel in the feeling of being there!

Repeating the words "Thank you, thank you, thank you, thank you, thank you" over and over again to your Spirit for guiding you home moves you more and more fully into the sub-

Breathe...Relax...Allow...Enjoy

lime realm of Easy World. Enjoy being ensconced in the Design for Harmony, in the embrace of your Spirit, at home in Easy World!

Honor your intuition as to what else you need to do. Your intuition is your Spirit guiding you.

Repeat as needed. (Know that if you are in the midst of a problem, you may well need to repeat the process. Just be patient—*nonresistant*—with yourself!)

FREQUENCY-RAISING SUPPORT TOOLS AND TECHNIQUES

The following are some of the many tools and energy-moving techniques that will help you bypass the Difficult World Dictator and get back to Easy World. By embracing these and allowing them to do their magic, you move out of resistance. Use these as part of Step Four, or anytime you need a lift:

- **Music** is one of the easiest, most effective passive tools for frequency raising. It's one I'm sure you've been instinctively using to uplift yourself all along. As long as it is chosen based on its being a match for your mood, it bypasses ego resistance and entrains your energy to it without effort.

  Once your ego has expressed itself and you're feeling more peaceful and ready to allow yourself to move toward joy, choose some music to boost you—*something that matches the mood*

Breathe...Relax...Allow...Enjoy

you're currently in. It will take you from where you are to the next level. Don't try to push the process with music that's too upbeat for your current mood; wait till you're really feeling it, and *then* let go to your all-out joy music! Singing along with and dancing to the music increases its power exponentially.

You may want to make and keep a playlist of music that is particularly effective at moving you higher, starting with some that meets you at a more somber place and then adding selections that help you ramp up to full-out joy. Joyful music was created in Easy World, and thus connects you with it!

- **Conscious breathing**—breathing dynamically and purposefully—realigns you with the rhythm of the Design for Harmony. One extremely simple but powerful technique is to imagine you are (a) breathing in Love, (b) circulating it throughout your body, where it not only infuses your cells but "liquefies" any energy blockages, turning them back into Love, and (c) exhaling this Love while imagining that it is blessing all Creation. Imagine as you do this that each Love-filled breath is taking you higher on the vibrational scale.

  Another extremely powerful exercise is to use circular breathing techniques (such as that used in rebirthing breathwork) to rapidly move energy blockages through and out and free your energy to flow. This technique consists of breathing evenly in and out through your mouth without a pause between inhale and exhale (make sure you're sitting or lying down). While it's definitely recommended that you have a coach certified in breathwork to supervise longer sessions of this, I have been able to raise my

Breathe...Relax...Allow...Enjoy

vibration very rapidly and safely on my own by doing it for only ten minutes.

- **Aromatherapy** is a powerful passive frequency raiser that easily and immediately bypasses all ego resistance—definitely an Easy World tool! All you have to do is take a sniff of a pure, natural fragrance, and you're there. The volatile, aromatic essences of plants were provided by the Creator for the purpose of assisting us in realigning with Source, thus balancing, healing, and energizing us and moving us into Easy World.

  Smelling a pleasant, pure plant fragrance or blend of fragrances brings our energy out of the reptilian brain and into the frontal lobes, where our more enlightened thinking takes place. Many fragrances, such as frankincense, sandalwood, rose, and balsam fir, are particularly effective for stimulating the pineal gland, where the experience of our direct connection with Source is accessed.

  Essential oils must be pure and distilled at a low temperature and at low pressure to maintain all their therapeutic properties. Artificial fragrances, such as commercial air fresheners, most perfumes, scented toiletries, and laundry products, not only do not have a therapeutic effect, but they also stress the body. If you don't have therapeutic-quality oils but have access to living plants that are fragrant, such as herbs and flowers, or other aromatic plant materials such as citrus peel or evergreen needles, simply crush them slightly and sniff them for a quick lift!

- **Soothing your solar plexus** when the Difficult World Dictator seems to have taken up residence there can go a long way toward

Breathe...Relax...Allow...Enjoy

helping you get back to Easy World. The solar plexus chakra (energy center) is located just below your sternum. When ego is in residence there, you may feel the sensation commonly referred to as a "knot in your stomach."

Breathing into the tension there and breathing it out while mentally directing it to relax and open can be helpful. Another technique to try is gently massaging the spot in a circular motion in whichever direction brings you relief (you'll likely be able to tell immediately which one helps, and which makes it feel worse!).

I have found aromatherapy to be powerfully helpful for untying the solar plexus knots I have so often found myself with. "Release," the essential oil blend I use for this, contains ylang-ylang, lavender, geranium, sandalwood, and blue tansy oils, and I massage it in as well as inhaling the aroma. This works like a charm for me! (You can find out more about this and the other blends I use at www.JuliaRogersHamrick.com at the "Energy Tools" link.) Only use therapeutic-quality essential oils on your skin and dilute them with pure, organic vegetable oil as needed.

Toning, which I talk about below in the "Vocalizing" section, is also effective for bringing the solar plexus back into balance, as is using a crystal singing bowl or other such instrument, tuned to the key of E. (Recordings of these will also work.)

- **Relaxation** is like "neutral" in the gears of a car. When we relax, we drop resistance and allow the immense magnetic pull of Easy World to draw us back into it. That's why two of the key actions we take after invoking Easy World are to *relax* and *allow.*

Breathe...Relax...Allow...Enjoy

If you find yourself out of Easy World, there is a great likelihood that you are experiencing muscle tension. Find a way to release that, first by simply recognizing it and consciously letting it go; just being conscious of it is the first step to relaxation. Try utilizing some of the many tools available to help with it.

Massage, preferably from another human being, will certainly help to bring you back to Easy World, but if you're on your own, using massage tools you operate yourself can help. I wouldn't be without my foot massagers, the trigger-point releaser for my back, and my handheld electric percussion massager for all over. I also massage my scalp and the reflex points on my feet and hands when I need to relax. When you release the tension in your muscles, your mind is bound to relax as well—and vice versa.

Using your breath to release tension is also a powerful tool for relaxing. Actually, all the tools and techniques on this list bring you to a more relaxed, nonresistant state, which could at least partially explain their vibration-raising magic.

And never underestimate the power of a nap to raise your frequency. We'll discuss why sleep is so healing and uplifting a little farther along in the book!

- **Vocalizing** not only moves energy through sound, it also engages the power of the breath. From moaning and groaning when you need to release stress, to singing or shouting for joy, chanting and toning for spiritual attunement, or speaking words of truth and Love, the human voice is an instrument created for moving energy through us, keeping us in balance, connected with Source and one another.

Breathe...Relax...Allow...Enjoy

While vocalization with words is balancing to both sides of your brain, wordless vocalizing rapidly bypasses ego. One of the most powerful ways I know to move higher is by *toning*. Toning—sounding a note with no words—is something you do spontaneously and instinctively as a child.

There are infinite ways to tone, but here is a technique to try: Start by sounding "ooooooooooo" (rhymes with "glue" and "shoe") at the lowest note your voice will go and raising the tone up smoothly over a period of a few seconds, from as low as you can easily go to as high as you can easily go, like a siren starting up, and hold the highest note as long as you can. *Do not force the sound—let your voice gently wrap around it so as not to cause vocal strain.* Repeat. Experiment with your voice and find your own favorite technique.

- **Exercising,** including stretching, is a really effective way to open up the energy pathways and get the Life Force flowing freely through your body again to raise your vibrational frequency. Your body was designed to move energy and be in motion. Physical movement not only causes energy and oxygen to move through your body and oxygenate your cells and clear your mind, it also stimulates the release of endorphins—the "happy hormones," which are obviously related to frequency raising because they accompany joy.

Whenever I am preparing, for example, to do a talk, or to write, and especially need clarity and wisdom, I swim vigorously for thirty to forty minutes nonstop. The movement, the oxygenation, and being in the water add up to my reaching a much higher vibrational state, with the clarity and wisdom that come along with it. In fact, whenever I'm feeling challenged to stay in Easy World, I swim.

I swim because that's the exercise I love to do, but any aerobic exercise *you* enjoy will be right for *you*. So do your favorite workout, dance, ride your bicycle, play a game that requires movement, or simply take a walk. Whatever you decide to do, the key is to *move*—move yourself right into Easy World!

- **Appreciation** puts you into alignment because it means you are not in resistance. You can't wholeheartedly appreciate something and be in resistance at the same time. When you actively appreciate something—anything—you automatically move higher on the scale because your evolved inner masculine self is in residence in your left brain instead of the critical, judgmental ego. This means you are in proper alignment so that Love can flow.

Writing a list of what you appreciate and why is an excellent tool for climbing the vibrational ladder. Writing a note to someone to express appreciation—even to tell her something as simple as that her smile is a blessing—is an uplifting exercise that also serves to help uplift the recipient. Gratitude is an especially powerful form of appreciation. Making a practice of expressing gratitude for everything in your life will help keep you in alignment, or bring you back when you've wandered into Difficult World.

You might want to keep a gratitude journal, or simply list in your mind what you're grateful for before you go to sleep each

Breathe...Relax...Allow...Enjoy

night or when you wake in the morning. Taking a "gratitude break" in the midst of a hectic day can rapidly bring you back to Easy World. Gratitude for anything is potent; offering gratitude for Easy World, even when you feel miles away from it, can help you find yourself at home in the blink of an eye!

- **Being in Nature** and allowing it to trigger your Love response to it is an amazing passive frequency raiser. Mother Nature really knows how to get your energy flowing—she draws it out of you. Simply being in Nature itself is uplifting, but adding appreciation to the mix is like rocket fuel for your return to Easy World.

Appreciate the ease with which a plant grows—even finding its way through concrete—effortlessly, without struggle or concern. Appreciate how breathtaking a flowering tree is in the spring without having spent any time at all in an effort to be something it's not, or any energy trying to look better than the tree next to it. Appreciate how squirrels gather food for the winter without first going to an office or a factory to make money, and without spending a dime at the grocery store. They live in Easy World full-time.

Even when things happen in Nature that we judge to be bad, the creatures in the natural world don't judge, and thus, they stay in Easy World. While we can readily see the deleterious effects that human beings in Difficult World have had on Nature, Nature actually exemplifies Easy World perfectly, and when you allow it to, it will pull you back into Easy World. Notice that when you find yourself back in Easy World, you see only beauty

Breathe...Relax...Allow...Enjoy

and perfection in Nature, because Difficult World effects are not present in EW.

- **Interacting with water,** a magical, electromagnetic substance, is a frequency raiser. Soaking in it, showering in it, swimming in it, gazing at it, drinking it, or however else you can think to engage with it, raises your vibration.

  Offering gratitude to water further boosts your frequency, and if you offer gratitude and think loving thoughts as you're holding water you're about to drink, you may find that it lifts you even higher as you partake of it.

  Being near water that is moving, such as by a waterfall, at the ocean's edge, next to a fountain, or even in your shower, exposes you to negative ions, which have an enlivening effect, causing endorphin release, balancing serotonin levels, and creating a sense of greater well-being. Most of my profound insights have occurred while I was showering, swimming, or gazing at a body of water.

- **Communing with the sun** is one of the most effective frequency boosters I know of. Its life-giving rays provide us with all we need to be physically embodied, spiritual beings on Planet Earth. My experience is that my vibration is naturally much higher on sunny days.

  When I need a boost, I like to go outside and turn my face to the sun and "look at it" *with my eyes closed,* letting the rays fall on my skin and turning my palms up to the sun. (I heard once that your palms absorb energy from sunlight, and I can feel a pulsing in my palms when I do this.) If you can expose your solar plexus to the sun and shine the light on the DWD's hide-out, even better!

If you are out in the direct sun for only fifteen to twenty min-utes, my feeling is that you don't risk sun damage and you will find yourself feeling recharged. Follow your own guidance on sun exposure and the use of sunscreen, but for such a short time, my sense of things is that unless you have a specific skin condition that requires it, protection is not needed and using it may keep you from receiving all the sun's benefits.

- **Writing** is a highly effective way to get the flow going so you move higher in frequency and closer to Easy World. As men-tioned in Step Three of the Step-by-Step Frequency-Raising Sys-tem, putting your feelings on paper removes blockages to the flow by letting ego express itself. From there, you can move on to expressing your more evolved feelings and truths. As you write, you will find yourself automatically feeling clearer and at a higher vibration.

Reaching up to your Spirit through writing a letter to express your prayers is a highly effective focusing device and one I use frequently when I'm out of Easy World, feeling lost or discon-nected. Writing a letter from your Spirit to you—perhaps in response to what you wrote in your letter to your Spirit—channeling your Spirit's totally loving, totally wise answer in response, moves you rapidly into alignment.

Anytime you consciously, purposefully reach up to the level where your Spirit's wisdom is, you move higher on the scale. Indeed, any kind of inspired writing brings your mind into

Breathe...Relax...Allow...Enjoy

focus, engaging your left brain in an activity serving your Spirit, and ensures it's not available for ego's use, thus moving you out of resistance. I think that's the main reason I love writing books and articles—it takes me higher and keeps me in Easy World!

- **Radiating Love unconditionally** is the most frequency-raising activity of all, because in order to do it, you have to be in alignment with Source! When you radiate Love *impersonally,* just the way Source does, without concern for who is receiving or appreciating it, you are automatically in perfect alignment.

It simply can't be done unless you are, since Source is where the Love comes from, and your alignment with Source opens the "pipe" so it can move through you. Radiating Love naturally locks out the DWD because while you're doing it, the action-oriented left brain is busy in service to Spirit and thus is unavailable to the fearful ego.

Even though we've forgotten this while we've been caught up in Difficult World, the ability to radiate Love is "hardwired" into us because doing so is what keeps us at the vibrational level of Easy World, where we were designed to thrive. Simply focus on your heart center, feel the energy welling up there, and just as the sun radiates light in all directions from its core, imagine Love radiating from your heart center out in all directions at once.

Don't "aim" it at anyone or anything because doing so brings the ego into it, and that takes you out of alignment. Keep your mind busy with making sure the Love continues to radiate. Practice doing this for ten seconds at a time and increasing it incrementally. Ideally, you'll be doing it constantly no matter what other activities you're engaged in—kind of like a program running in the background on your computer. If you consistently radiate Love unconditionally, you will always be in Easy World!

This is by no means a comprehensive list of the tools and techniques that will help you raise your vibrational frequency to return to Easy World. And they are not just tools to use when you find yourself down and in the DWD's grip. They are tools to integrate into your daily life.

There are some that are specific to you that you can add to the list. And you certainly won't need to use all of these at any one time. After you've done one or two of them, you'll most likely be back in Easy World, feeling great again.

I suggest you go ahead and try out the techniques you've never used so that when you find yourself in need of the Step-by-Step Frequency-Raising System, you will have already experienced them and will not have to figure them out when the DWD is in charge—I'm sure you've experienced how much fun it is to try something new when He Who Makes Things Difficult is calling the shots!

What If It Doesn't Work?

Yes, raising your vibration and getting back to Easy World is the way to resolve any problem and move from sadness, disappoint-

Breathe...Relax...Allow...Enjoy

ment, and even shock back to joy. It *will* work, given enough focus and time. But how in heaven's name do you do this when your dreams have been shattered? When someone you love is gone? When something violent has happened? When you don't know where your next meal is coming from? When all your resources seem to have dried up? When you're too weak or depressed or sick to do anything? When you're having a "dark night of the soul"?

There may be times when the resistance is so strong—when what is happening is so overwhelming—that you may feel unable to do anything beyond simply surviving.

Something remarkable I have personally experienced is that when you are absolutely bereft and out of ideas and energy, rock bottom is a truly powerful place to be, though it may feel anything but. When you are there, the illusion that you, at the human-ego level, can control what happens is stripped away. And that means you are ready to let your Spirit lead.

If you find yourself in such a dark, fearful place that you can't bring yourself to take any other action, when you can't even muster the energy to apply the Step-by-Step System, there *is* something powerful you can do that takes no energy at all: just surrender—or, at least, express your intent to do so.

Surrender is the ultimate act of nonresistance and the most empowering act of all. It puts you back in proper alignment immediately.

Like my experience in Japan that I related in Chapter 4— the one where I was totally stymied by a problem I couldn't

Breathe...Relax...Allow...Enjoy

solve, had the giant meltdown, and then started experiencing miracles—when you are at rock bottom, you are stripped down to your essence, and therein lies your power. That is when you *surrender*. You surrender to your Spirit and turn everything over to the one who is always completely devoted to your well-being, knows exactly what you need, and can lead you back to the heart of the Design for Harmony, where problems are solved.

When you're ready to "give up" (give your situation *up* to a higher power) and let your Spirit take over, you will find yourself in Easy World again. But you must be ready to. Oftentimes, we need to wallow in Difficult World awhile before we're ready to let go, relax, and slip out of the trap. That's perfect, actually. Wallowing is just a form of allowing—it even has the word *allow* within it! Remember Step Three in the Step-by-Step Frequency-Raising System? Basically, it's about deliberately wallowing as a way to release resistance.

When your *intention* is getting back to Easy World—back to peace and, as unthinkable as it may seem when you're in the midst of a serious situation, back to *joy*—whatever allowing you do in any form will move you in that direction. The more you express your intent to surrender and let go as best you can, the higher you'll climb, even if sometimes it's just millimeters at a time.

Be patient with yourself. Remember, impatience simply feeds the Difficult World Dictator. Be kind and compassionate with yourself—that *really* puts the DWD in his place!

Breathe...Relax...Allow...Enjoy

When you're ready to allow yourself to be there, to drop re-sistance to being in the embrace of Easy World, you'll find yourself ensconced in the Design for Harmony once again, feeling the joy that is your birthright. Your intention is a pow-erful thing.

Your solutions, your blessings, and your joy are waiting for you in Easy World. Don't let the Difficult World Dictator keep you from them!

Next, let's look at more of the countless ways choosing Easy World transforms and betters your life.

I choose to live in Easy World,

where everything is easy.

Breathe...Relax...Allow...Enjoy

8

Thriving in Your
Easy World Life

I bet I don't even have to tell you that by your choosing Easy World, your life is going to change in amazing and thrilling ways—but I'm going to anyway. If you decide that living an Easy World life is for you, be prepared to greatly increase your capacity for ease, joy, fulfillment, prosperity, and magic!

Every area of your life is about to be upgraded, from the parts you're not too pleased with to the parts you think are pretty swell already. Even the aspects you've decided are hopeless will transform! From the big stuff to the small stuff, Easy World handles it all, effortlessly, efficiently, and effectively. Easy World is where you were designed to thrive.

Even though it's an impossible undertaking to try to list—or even conceive of—all the specific ways in which choosing Easy World will impact your experience of life, I do want to give you

Breathe...Relax...Allow...Enjoy

at least a taste. So let's look at some of the areas that seem to matter most to us and at least touch on how living an Easy World life can impact them.

BEING YOUR SELF AT LAST

Your Self, spelled with a capital "S," is the you that is determined by your own true nature rather than the person you have created by conforming to external ideas of what you ought to be and do. Your Self is the authentic version of you that follows your own Spirit and lives in alignment with the Design for Harmony. You might say it's your Easy World Self—the one you started out being and the one you're becoming again.

One of the most empowering gifts of Easy World—perhaps *the* most empowering—is that Easy World allows you to be your Self and to experience the untold blessings of that. In fact, you might even say Easy World *demands* that you be your Self. It not only allows you to align with your natural preferences, desires, and energy and gives you permission not to be or do what anyone else thinks you ought to be or do, it requires it.

To do otherwise means you're not in Easy World.

When you base your thoughts and actions on anything other than your own divine guidance system, you automatically move into Difficult World. When you deny your own pleasure and joy, you are in Difficult World. When you try to be anyone but the authentic you, you are in Difficult World. But when you honor your Self, you are in Easy World.

Breathe...Relax...Allow...Enjoy

Honoring your Self is a big part of being in Easy World because that is how you stay aligned with the Design for Harmony. Being aligned with the Design for Harmony is how you receive all the blessings that only a system designed to support your total well-being can offer.

Needless to say, being your Self is *not* supported in Difficult World. Making sure that you are denying your inner guidance and are listening to voices other than your Spirit's is how the Difficult World Dictator ensures that you stay aligned with the Design for *Dis*harmony. It is a highly effective method, and the DWD counts on it. If he can keep you from being your Self, he will always have plenty of misery to feed off of.

Most of us—actually, probably *all* of us—have been in some degree of lifelong pain because of the discrepancy between who we really are and what we've become by denying our own inner guidance system. It has pained us to abandon our Selves and that which we deeply, naturally desire to be and, instead, do what we've thought we *had* to in order to achieve success as a human being, or even simply to survive.

We've been had! Abandoning our Selves is not a recipe for success or survival. It's a recipe for pain and suffering, and ultimately, death. It's a guarantee of being in Difficult World. There's no real success in DW, only the illusion of it. *Real success—happiness and fulfillment—is not a feature of Difficult World*. Real success is found only in Easy World.

To experience the fulfillment human beings are always chasing in DW, you need to be in Easy World. To be in Easy World, you need to be your Self.

The relief of this—the energy it will free up, and the ripple effect it will have in your life—is impossible to calculate. At last, not only do you have permission to be Who You Really Are, but Easy World also rewards you for being your Self with blessings beyond measure.

DISCOVERING YOUR PURPOSE AND FULFILLING IT

Have you been seeking your unique reason for being—your personal mission? Do you feel a powerful desire to make some sort of meaningful contribution to your world, one that is personal to you? One of the benefits of being your Self is that it will make clear to you the things you were designed to do because they are the activities that will be most fulfilling to you. Being your Self will point you to your divine purpose and ensure that you are able to fulfill it.

Easy World is where you were designed to be the most successful you can possibly be. Fulfilling your purpose is a key part of being authentically successful. When you have discovered and are fulfilling your purpose, everything else just lines up for you because you are in alignment with the Design for Harmony. Likewise, when you are in alignment with the Design for Harmony, finding your purpose happens naturally!

Breathe...Relax...Allow...Enjoy

The Design for Harmony provides definite clues as to when you've found your perfect place within it. You will feel a greater flow of Love when you're there. That means you've clicked into alignment with the Design for Harmony and, therefore, the Love/Life Force is flowing freely within you and lifting you up. That which is aligned with your true purpose will always trigger an experience consistent with a greater flow of Love.

Thus, when you're loving doing something—when you feel an increase of energy when you're doing something—pay attention! It means you're in Easy World, and in your place in the Design. This positions you to experience even more Love, joy, prosperity, and fulfillment because those are the rewards of being in alignment with the Design for Harmony. It's quite an amazing system. Be your Self and do what you were designed to do and you hit the jackpot!

The one and only reason people miss finding and fulfilling their true purpose is that they let their fearful egos dictate their actions and keep them entrenched in the Design for *Dis*harmony, and out of the Design for Harmony. They don't get around to doing what they love to do because they are too busy in Difficult World, doing what they think they *have* to do to make money, impress people, and so on.

It is somewhat mind-boggling to imagine the convoluted journey we've taken from doing what we love to do in Easy World—what is a perfect fit for our talents and passion and that prospers us as well as the Whole—to doing what we don't particularly like to do, but think we *have* to do in order to pay

Breathe...Relax...Allow...Enjoy

the bills in Difficult World. That Difficult World Dictator is quite the con artist!

When you're in Easy World, it is not possible for you to fill your time with things you don't like to do or distract yourself from your true purpose with work you've undertaken out of fear you won't be able to survive unless you do it. That's Difficult World! Being in Easy World means you are in alignment with your Spirit, ensconced in the Design for Harmony, and doing that which catalyzes joy in your experience.

You may be reading this and thinking about how your current job was a Difficult World choice and that it is keeping you in Difficult World. If you're wondering how you're ever going to bridge the gap between your current job and doing that which is aligned with your purpose, take heart!

Even if you're currently doing something just to make money, or for any other reason not fully aligned with the Design for Harmony, keep choosing Easy World, and you will automatically start the process of making a change in your situation. Easy World will easily and sequentially guide you more and more closely to your place in the Design. It will happen naturally. You just have to *start where you are* and let Easy World do all the heavy lifting.

Being in Easy World can be accomplished no matter where you find yourself. The DWD may tell you that there's no way you can be in Easy World while you're doing a job you don't love, but consider who is telling you that! Choosing Easy World no matter where you are or what you're doing makes

Breathe...Relax...Allow...Enjoy

any situation harmonious. Doing so will transform your experience. All your circumstances will evolve to support being more closely aligned with the Design for Harmony.

The more time you spend in Easy World, the more clear your unique purpose will become, the closer you'll come to fulfilling it, and the more truly prosperous, harmonious, joy-filled, and, of course, *easier* your life will be.

TRUE PROSPERITY IS FOUND ONLY IN EASY WORLD

The natural result of living an Easy World life, being your Self, fulfilling your purpose, and doing what you love to do is *prosperity*.

Before continuing, let me define true prosperity for you. Being truly prosperous is having the peace of mind and the empowered feeling that come from knowing that everything you need and desire is always available to you when you need and want it with 100 percent reliability. True prosperity is a function of being in Easy World, where everything is provided for you effortlessly, efficiently, and exactly at the right time—not before, not after, but exactly when you need it.

True prosperity is not having a stockpile of money—that's a Difficult World notion. It's certainly what your fearful ego wants and tells you that you must have, but it's not reliable. Stockpiles can be depleted, stolen, or devalued. They are not secure.

Easy World, on the other hand, is absolutely secure. It's the only

Breathe...Relax...Allow...Enjoy

truly secure investment there is! And just to be clear about money and Easy World, it may well be that you'll have a pile of money in Easy World. But it won't be for security's sake, or because your fearful ego needs it. It will be for your sheer enjoyment.

The bottom line on money is that it represents power. You are as powerful as it's possible to be when you're in Easy World. You can have everything you desire in Easy World with or without money. Easy World is perfectly efficient and does not need to use money as an intermediary to deliver all that you need and desire. I can hardly wait till you experience the magic of getting what you desire in Easy World without paying a cent! It's happened to me over and over again, and I still get a thrill from it. You will, too.

You were designed to live in total prosperity. That's why you long for it, and feel so cheated when you don't have it. From the beginning, your Creator set things up so that you would al-ways—*always*—be perfectly provided for without struggle. The Master Mind created Easy World for you so that you would have everything you could ever need or want, *as long as you're there.*

That's the catch—the only one. To have everything you could ever need or want, you have to be in Easy World. You can't have Easy World benefits while you're in Difficult World. You have to go to EW to get them. Staying in Difficult World is like hav-ing a million bucks in the other room but refusing to go get it, all the while complaining about not having any money!

Let me reiterate: *When you choose Easy World, everything you need or desire is already yours. All you have to do is show up and claim it.* You may have forgotten it, but nevertheless, it continues

Breathe...Relax...Allow...Enjoy

to be true. Your Spirit has already seen to your needs—your desires, too. You are fabulously wealthy in Easy World.

If you are familiar with the New Testament of the Bible, you may remember that in Matthew 6:33, it is reported that the master teacher, Jesus, when discussing the various needs and wants of the people, said, "Seek ye first the kingdom of God, and all these things shall be added unto you."

Although it was expressed in language from a different time, I am quite sure Jesus was talking about Easy World.

He was talking about the creative matrix that has been provided for you as your ultra-easy manifestation place, where all you have to do is think of what you need and it's yours, where it's yours even before you realize you need or want it—you just have to claim it! He was talking about the realm of your Spirit, which is Easy World.

While I'm sure biblical scholars would object, I would paraphrase his words as "Choose Easy World first, and there you will have everything you need and want."

So many of us get hung up on prosperity issues—on trying to obtain what we believe we need. The truth of the matter is that what we're trying so desperately to manifest is already ours in Easy World! Would you believe that if you don't have what you're desiring, it's probably because you're trying too hard? Or worrying about not being able to get it? Or looking for it in the wrong place?

If you don't have what you truly desire, it's because you're trying to find your Easy World treasure in Difficult World.

Breathe...Relax...Allow...Enjoy

To receive these limitless blessings, you need to follow the Law of Easy World: *Worry, strife, and struggle, in any form, are strictly prohibited.* Your job is not to *make* things happen; your job is to *allow* them to. Your job is not to figure out *how* to get what you want, your job is to be in touch with your desires, be relaxed and ready to respond to inspiration and energy, do as you are guided to, and know where to pick up your blessings when the time is right!

Easy World is Prosperity Central.

DESIRE? OR WANT?

For clarity, I need to define a couple of things for you. While I realize not everyone defines these terms as I do, I want you to understand what *I* mean by them.

My definition of a "desire" is something you'd love to have that is aligned with and implanted in your awareness by your Spirit. Essentially, it's an announcement that something perfect for you—something life-enhancing—is ready to be claimed. Where do you claim it? In Easy World, of course.

A "want," on the other hand, is aligned with your fearful ego and signifies that you lack something. A want is a hole the DWD creates to suck you into. A want is a diversion from Easy World. A want says you don't have something. But in Easy World, you have everything. Well, *almost* everything.

I think it's important to let you know that while you can have anything you *desire,* your ego-based *wants* are not supported in

Breathe...Relax...Allow...Enjoy

Easy World. Remember that your Spirit, your Easy World guide and administrator, has your well-being in mind at all times. It knows everything about you and what you need, and what will fulfill you and bring you joy, as well as what will move your life toward even *more* joy. That is your Spirit's priority.

The Difficult World Dictator, however, as you now well know, is in business for himself. The DWD has a vested interest in keeping you frustrated and unhappy, so anything he comes up with as a want will ultimately just contribute to your frustration and unhappiness.

Basically, if something you think you want is not in alignment with the Design for Harmony, it will not be yours in Easy World. If it *is* in alignment with the Design for Harmony, it will be. If something is not in alignment with the Design for Harmony, you will be better off without it—unless you haven't yet had your fill of painful, Difficult World adventures!

It's a remarkable and elegantly simple system. Align with the Design, and you easily have it all.

RELATIONSHIPS THRIVE IN EASY WORLD

One of the blessings we human beings all seem to most long for is one-on-one partnership and romantic love.* Though some of us have discovered that entering into such a partnership is like

---

*Note the use of the lowercase "l" here to connote "in love" as a perceived state of being rather than the capital "L" used for "Love," the essence of Life.

Breathe...Relax...Allow...Enjoy

asking to be catapulted into Difficult World, and we've experienced more hurt than joy from these relationships, we still crave them and seek them over and over again. Why is this?

It's because since we originally departed from Easy World, we have largely been missing the feeling of Oneness that is the hallmark of our true home. We all long to feel the union we felt before we let the Difficult World Dictator deceive us into believing we are all separate, competitive entities instead of facets of a unified Whole.

So, we seek relationships with others as a way to try to fulfill that longing for Oneness. But most of us quickly find that the longing is fulfilled only briefly before "reality" sets in. You meet someone who turns you on, they are just as attracted to you, everything is rosy, you feel whole and complete, everything about your new beloved is perfect, and the whole world looks different—fresh, new, and wonderful.

It's like being in Paradise. Then, next thing you know, the bloom is off the rose. Issues come up and things get complicated. Before long, Oneness is the last thing your relationship is reminiscent of, and Paradise is the last place you feel you are.

So, what's up with that?

When you are newly in love, something about the other person lulls your fearful ego into dropping his barriers so that he is not resisting the flow of Love in and through you. Love is flowing at optimal levels, your vibrational frequency shoots way up, and you feel joy—ecstasy, even. Everything is perfect! Your vibrational level is now right up there with that of Easy World, of

Breathe...Relax...Allow...Enjoy

Paradise. Thus, the reality that is evident to you at that point is that of Easy World.

The enlivened, exhilarated, blissful way you feel and the way everything and everyone—especially your partner—is so beautiful and perfect when you're newly in love is what Easy World is like all the time! (Granted, few of us are spending enough time in Easy World at this point to get the full effect, but that is the potential; I have experienced it.)

But soon this rarefied experience of being in love fades and your experience changes. One reason is that the Difficult World Dictator is shocked into waking up when he realizes that this union—this new level of being—is threatening his very existence, and he jumps in and asserts himself. He begins pointing out differences, likes and dislikes, and so on, and uses those to get you to resist allowing Love to flow freely.

As he blocks the flow of Love, you sink back down to the vibrational level of Difficult World, just where he wants you. As he continues his campaign to prevent you from experiencing the Oneness that threatens him, he keeps you dwelling on differences and issues that divide. All the things about the other person that you then decide you don't like begin to be prominent in your awareness. Conflict sets in. You're in Difficult World, land of separation.

Difficult World separates; Easy World unifies. Clashes happen in DW; harmony happens in EW.

Therefore, in order to stay "in love," you need to stay in *Love*! You need to choose Easy World as many times as it takes

Breathe...Relax...Allow...Enjoy

to keep the Love flowing fully and freely through you so that you stay at a higher vibrational level, where harmony reigns and all is joyful.

That way, your view will be that of beauty and perfection instead of ugliness and flaws. That way, you feel at one with the other person, and you feel whole. It's the wholeness you're longing for. But it cannot be found in another person—it is found in Easy World, in the Design for Harmony that is the foundation for EW.

We've misunderstood that wholeness thing. We've been looking for completion in another person—in other people— but the feeling of completion happens only when you're in Easy World. Being at one with your Spirit triggers the feeling you're missing. Being in Easy World provides the sense that you're whole.

It's never the other person that makes you feel whole, it's the reality state. It's plugging in to the Design for Harmony (which I have also been known to call the "Design for Wholeness and Harmony") that gives you the feeling of completeness. It's being where you belong, in the embrace of your Spirit, in harmony with all of Creation. That's the way to feel whole.

Whether they're conscious of it or not, other people innately know that they are not capable of making you feel whole, so they are repelled by your attempts to find wholeness through being with them. If you don't understand this, you are even more vulnerable to relationship problems, fueled, of course, by the DWD.

Breathe...Relax...Allow...Enjoy

You will always feel alone and separate in Difficult World, the Land of the Illusion of Separateness. But you will always feel whole when you're in Easy World. It's the Land of Wholeness! In EW, it is irrelevant whether you are intimately involved with another human being or not—you simply feel whole and fulfilled.

When you feel whole, fulfilled, and joyful no matter who is sharing your life, the Law of Attraction will draw to you other human beings who feel whole, fulfilled, and joyful. That's the foundation for healthy, happy relationships. Even if you've been in a relationship for sixty years, choosing Easy World can transform it.

I know this begs the question "What if the other person isn't in Easy World?" It matters not what any other person's perceptions of his or her reality are. *When you are in Easy World, everyone you encounter is in Easy World with you.* If you notice that the other person is not happy, or that things between you are not harmonious, or just that the other person is in Difficult World, it means that *you've* slipped out of Easy World!

You, and you alone, determine what you experience by virtue of which channel you're tuned to. *You* are responsible for staying in Easy World. Any way you slice it, if you want company to play with you in Easy World, it's up to you.

If you don't already have a life partner and you desire one, the way to attract and create a relationship that is healthy and just right for you is by being in Easy World. As someone who was married at twenty-three and then was single again from age twenty-five to age forty-four, I would have loved to have known about Easy World so that I could have deliberately used that knowledge to create a healthy partnership. I didn't.

Fortunately, however, I had learned to trust and follow my Spirit's guidance, and that's virtually the same as choosing Easy World. One of my most remarkable Easy World experiences happened before I made my official EW discovery. I think you'll agree that it could only have happened in Easy World. . . .

As of early autumn 1997, it had been almost eighteen years since my first husband and I divorced, nine years since my last serious boyfriend, and eight years since my last real date. While I longed for partnership, and had made list after list of the qualities I wanted in a mate, I always added "someday" to my thoughts about being with that special man of my longings.

You see, like pretty much everyone else, I had experienced pain in relationships because of limiting beliefs and unhealthy behavioral patterns taken on in my Difficult World sojourn, and I was determined to protect myself from more pain. I had been intently "working on myself" for many years, doing all I knew how to do to clear out old, damaging belief systems, to grow spiritually, and to heal myself so that the next relationship I would create would be healthy and harmonious.

I was not about to open myself to a relationship until I felt I was no longer vulnerable to the old patterns at the roots of my past relationship problems, and no longer vulnerable to the old pain. Even though I was at the pinnacle of my physical attractiveness, I had not even had one nibble in eight years, nor felt

Breathe...Relax...Allow...Enjoy

even a mild heart flutter! Sure, I'd had some male admiration, but no approaches. It was almost as if I were wearing a neon sign saying "Stay away!"

Truthfully, at the same time I was harboring a desire for partnership, the lack of male interest suited me just fine—it meant I was safe from relationship pain and heartache. Still, I continued to work on my list for that right man of the future. He would be intelligent, funny, kind, affectionate, easygoing, willing to grow, and on the same wavelength spiritually as I.

This last qualification was the kicker. Having a nowhere-near-mainstream spiritual perspective (as you may have noticed!), and not having found, at the time, anyone, male *or* female, who saw things the way that I did, I thought it would be quite impossible to find someone who would match up with me spiritually.

But that was an absolute requirement for me. Since I had little or no confidence that such a man could even exist, surely the chances of finding him, if by some miracle he did, were infinitesimal. (I hadn't yet realized the extent of my power to create my reality!) Every time I had such a thought, I would feel a bit overwhelmed, so I would just release the whole thing to my Spirit.

I'm not sure when I thought "the future" would be; not sure when I thought I'd feel sufficiently ready to open myself up to getting involved with someone. But trusting implicitly in my Spirit, I knew that when the time was right—if he was even out there—I would be guided to connect with him and I would face my fears then. That time came sooner than I expected. It came so fast, I never saw it coming.

Breathe...Relax...Allow...Enjoy

One evening, as I was finishing up a shopping errand in a large discount store, I wandered into their book section and found myself powerfully drawn to a book about conscious relationships—relationships built on shared spiritual awareness. It beckoned me almost as if it had a beacon embedded in it that was flashing my name, so I bought it and immediately immersed myself in it. I started it that night and finished it just after lunch the next day.

In reading it, I realized that being in a relationship with someone is like taking a graduate course in spiritual growth, and with spiritual growth being my prime focus, I suddenly recognized it was what I needed as my next step. I realized that there weren't enough years in a lifetime to effectively pain-proof yourself against being hurt in a relationship; as in every other aspect of my life, I just needed to trust my Spirit to guide me step-by-step, moment by moment. I knew if I did, all would be well.

As I turned the last page, I affirmed, if haltingly, to my Spirit, "I'm ready now to grow spiritually within an intimate partnership with a man." As I took my next breath, I felt something inside me shift, as if I'd clicked into another reality. Now I know that reality was Easy World.

Moments later, I went to my computer because the book had advertised an online forum for people interested in discussing the book's principles, and I was certainly eager to explore these ideas further. There, I spotted an interesting post from a nice man who lived in Denver. We began conversing via the forum and continued through e-mail. Miraculously, his spiritual

Breathe...Relax...Allow...Enjoy

understandings were so on par with mine that when I read an essay that he had written, I wondered if I, myself, had written it!

He had all the other qualifications, too—he was smart, funny, kind, affectionate, easygoing, and committed to growing spiritually. (I later found out he was also physically attractive!) We hit it off instantly.

After a couple of months of friendship and getting to know each other, it became clear that we belonged together, and we committed ourselves to each other. I moved across the country from North Carolina to be with him so he wouldn't have to be away from his young daughters.

Then, a year and a half after we met, Rick and I were married, and we have continued growing in love ever since.

Now, more than twelve years later, it still astonishes me how quickly and easily it all happened. There was no searching or struggling or further waiting involved. I told my Spirit—my personal Easy World guide—that I was ready for a relationship, and there it was! Only minutes after I stopped resisting and went into allowing mode, I met my life partner. I'd call that easy, wouldn't you?

So if you're ready to attract a partner—someone to enjoy life with, someone to grow spiritually with, someone to have Easy World adventures with (and, let's be realistic here, some Difficult World ones, too)—try doing what I did. Ask your personal Easy World guide to handle things for you, make sure you're in Easy World, and watch the magic unfold!

Breathe...Relax...Allow...Enjoy

It may not happen as quickly for you as it did for me, but it will certainly happen at the rate you're willing to allow it to, and in the time and manner that best fits with the Design for Harmony so as to support your well-being, and the well-being of your partner-to-be.

Meanwhile, choosing Easy World in every area of your life ensures that you are as happy and emotionally healthy as you can be. It guarantees that the relationships you attract and create are happy and emotionally healthy, too, whether with a romantic partner, your family members, or your friends. Feeling whole and in harmony with life the way you do in Easy World is the key to having the kind of easy, joyful, emotionally fulfilling relationships you long for.

And these principles apply to all human relationships, not just the romantic ones. We're seeking cooperation and harmony and that feeling of Oneness all the time, with everyone, even though we may not be consciously aware of it. And the DWD is seeking separation and disharmony all the time. So, to maintain harmony and be happy in all your relationships, it just makes sense to choose Easy World.

YOUR ULTIMATE HAPPY PLACE

Built into you is the deep and abiding desire for happiness. Indeed, at the foundation of everything else you may long for—relationships, prosperity, spiritual experiences, material

Breathe...Relax...Allow...Enjoy

things—is the underlying desire for joy. It is a vital part of your human design.

This longing for joy is your Creator's way of making sure that however deeply you immerse yourself in Difficult World, you'll always long for the realm of joy—Easy World, your true home.

Joy is a sort of homing device to guide you back to where you belong. When you experience joy, you know you are where you were designed to thrive. When you are not experiencing joy, you know you've slipped out of Easy World and back into Difficult World, where thriving is not at all what you experience.

Easy World is the realm of joy because it manifests at the vibrational frequency that automatically and naturally catalyzes joy within human beings. Joy is the feeling signature of Easy World. When you are at that vibration, you are joyful, and for no particular reason. You experience what I call *unconditional joy*—joy that happens for no external reason. That is your original state, and the one you return to when you choose Easy World.

The more time you spend in Easy World, the more joyful you'll become, making it even easier to stay in Easy World. Just as in the last chapter when I told you that my emotional and vibrational set points were elevated when I made a practice of deliberately raising my vibrational frequency, so will making a practice of choosing Easy World raise your emotional set point—the level of feeling you return to when the highs and lows level out.

Breathe...Relax...Allow...Enjoy

When you've spent enough time in Easy World and your set point has been sufficiently raised, you'll *default* to joy! This is the state of perpetual happiness you were designed to experience. This doesn't mean you can't revisit less-than-joy anytime you like—it just means that less-than-joy is a choice, not a requirement, the way the DWD has so very much wanted you to believe.

IT'S A PROCESS

The thought of continuous joy may be a bigger leap than you are ready to make at this point. After all, expanding your capacity for ease and joy is something of a process after having a Difficult World orientation for so long. So let's talk a bit more about what happens in the meantime, when you're straddling realities and still spending much of your time in Difficult World, but choosing Easy World more and more.

The more time you spend in Easy World, the less embroiled you'll be in Difficult World, *even when you're in it*. When you're in DW, you'll be *aware* that you're there instead of thinking it's just the way life is, period. You won't be as vulnerable to getting bogged down in the drama and trauma as you once might have been. You will no longer be fooled into thinking the holograms your fearful ego creates are real, even when they appear and even feel real.

And you won't stay as long now that you know you don't have to. Now that you've got the Difficult World Dictator's number,

Breathe...Relax...Allow...Enjoy

you will be better able to see through his machinations and absurd illusions and simply opt out. Now that you know to choose Easy World, and will have experienced the relief in doing that, it will become a habit and you'll find yourself choosing Easy World as a reflex.

One of the amazing things about choosing Easy World is that your entire life experience—physical, mental, emotional, and spiritual—will be upgraded as you give more and more of yourself to the process. The first time you deliberately choose Easy World, you set in motion a process of transformation that continues whether or not you're consciously aware of it.

By consistently choosing Easy World, you'll find that there's nothing else you need to do to facilitate the process of creating your Easy World life of peace, prosperity, and joy. It will unfold naturally and in whatever way best supports your total well-being. And to think—you've been working on yourself, trying to achieve spiritual and personal transformation and empowerment, when you could have just been choosing Easy World! Now you know.

FAITH IS NOT FOR THE FAINT OF HEART

Does relying on Easy World instead of participating in Difficult World behaviors like worry, manipulation, hard work, et cetera, require trusting in something outside the three-dimensional realm of ordinary awareness? Does it require faith? You bet.

Breathe...Relax...Allow...Enjoy

It requires faith that Easy World exists, faith that it is always supporting your ultimate well-being, and faith that everything is always working out harmoniously for you there. When you have total confidence in your personal Easy World guide's reliability in always, without fail, being on top of things (your Spirit never sleeps) and trust that everything you need is yours without struggle in Easy World, you will be rewarded with proof that this is so.

Such is the nature of faith. You have to have it first, before the evidence that your faith is justified will come. Where do you get faith?

You simply *decide* to have it. Your fearful ego will certainly try to prevent that. It will point out all the possible downsides of having faith that it can come up with. It will tell you how silly and naive you are—irresponsible, even. (Anything you can't measure with your five senses is always considered fair game for ridicule by your fearful ego.) It will continually try to get you to chuck your faith in Easy World and reinvest in its world of struggle. As usual, you'll just need to tune it out and, instead, tune in your Spirit's messages of Love and encouragement.

Sometimes, a little patience (something your ego-mind is woefully short on) is needed to align with Easy World's timing. So often the DWD jumps in and yanks you out of Easy World and out of the confident expectation of the fulfillment of your desire because something doesn't happen the minute you think it ought to. He takes advantage of that to get you back where he

Breathe...Relax...Allow...Enjoy

wants you—back where you won't even be able to see that your desire has been delivered in Easy World.

That's why it's vital to have total respect for the intelligence, rhythm, and timing of the Design for Harmony. You just need to hang loose and not get hung up on how things appear to be going.

Your Spirit, in coordination with the Design for Harmony, lines everything up for you in the optimal order and timing to coordinate with the Whole, and with your ultimate well-being— yours, and that of everyone and everything—factored in. You won't always see the workings of this, and when you do, it won't always make sense to you. So, instead of relying on external evidence to decide if things are going your way, you will need to just trust that they always are—in Easy World. They are.

Once you've persevered in having faith despite appearances, and you've experienced Easy World magic, having faith in it from then on will be a piece of cake! A true, unshakeable knowing that every aspect of your life is always being supported in Easy World is something that will develop as you continue to choose Easy World over and over again.

IF THIS SEEMS TO BE BACKFIRING

Though choosing Easy World absolutely makes your whole life far easier and much more delightful the more time you spend in it, it's important to consider that because you've spent so

Breathe...Relax...Allow...Enjoy

much of your life creating your reality in Difficult World, there are likely to be some challenging situations already on their way down the pike.

After so many years of fervently believing what your fearful ego has told you, things that just aren't true in Easy World, you may have already set in motion some things that are going to show up in your experience—your Difficult World experience, that is. Encountering them may make it seem as if you haven't made much progress in creating your new EW life. Don't be fooled. Bring them into Easy World with you and watch them transform.

In addition, upon seeing that you're slipping away from him, the Difficult World Dictator may decide to stir things up in an effort to lure you back into his clutches. He may step up the rate of his invitations back to DW at first. This can seem like backward motion, but it's not. It's actually a sign of progress. If you use these DW summonses as prompts to choose Easy World instead of resisting them or getting upset over them, you will find yourself experiencing joy again that much faster.

Abandoning Easy World will be completely counterproductive here. Only by continuing to choose Easy World can you effectively deal with any Difficult World situations that arise for any reason and lift your life up higher where problems are fewer and life is easier and more joyful.

Soon you'll be cruising in the calmer waters of your new, Easy World life. You'll be experiencing the problem-solving

Breathe...Relax...Allow...Enjoy

magic of Easy World, and you'll be reliably collecting the limit-less blessings that are already yours in Easy World. Before long, you'll be thriving in every way, just as you were created to.

I am so excited for you and all the wondrous experiences you're going to have by choosing Easy World!

I choose to live in Easy World,

where everything is easy.

Breathe...Relax...Allow...Enjoy

9

Supporting Your
Easy World Life

So you're now choosing Easy World, and you're experiencing its magic. Fantastic! To support your rebirth into a life of far greater ease and joy, there are things you can do that will help clear the way and create conditions conducive to your new Easy World way of living.

That's what this chapter is devoted to: giving you ideas for enhancing your transition from your old life to your new one, and supporting your Easy World experience going forward. These suggestions are optional, of course, and you'll simply utilize the ones that appeal to you—the ones you're guided to. Those will be of the most help because your attraction to them indicates that they are in alignment for you.

Be patient and kind with yourself during this process. You're a recovering Difficult World addict! Remember that impatience

Breathe...Relax...Allow...Enjoy

and unkindness are hallmarks of the DWD. If you get frustrated with yourself for not moving faster in your transformation—for falling back into Difficult World—you are simply setting yourself back.

Breathe . . . relax . . . allow . . . enjoy . . . and be your own number one supporter, cheerleader, and best friend! Then you can watch the magic that is your Easy World life unfold.

HELP YOURSELF REMEMBER TO CHOOSE EASY WORLD

There's a really excellent chance, even when your earnest intention is to be in Easy World, that you're going to continue to be seduced back into Difficult World. This will happen less often than before, and less and less often as you continue choosing Easy World, but until you form a strong, rote habit of choosing Easy World, you may find yourself *forgetting* to choose it, even when you need to the most!

To be sure that choosing Easy World doesn't just slip your mind, here are some things you can set up for yourself to help you remember:

- **Post notes in strategic places to remind yourself to choose Easy World.** Put them where you spend the most time—in your home, office, car, et cetera. They can say simply "Easy World!" or "I choose to live in Easy World, where everything is easy" or

Breathe . . . Relax . . . Allow . . . Enjoy

"Breathe . . . relax . . . allow . . . enjoy," or whatever will best trigger you to choose Easy World.

Handwritten signs, or ones designed on the computer, as plain or as fancy as you want to make them, will work great, or you can download some I designed. The Freebies page of my Easy World Web site, at www.ILiveInEasyWorld.com, has a wealth of free mini-posters and such that you can print out and post.

- **Create and post special, situation-specific reminders** in addition to your generic EW ones. I did this when I was seeking a publisher for *Choosing Easy World*. I made a mini-poster for myself, and I sent one to Lisa, my literary agent, as well.

    At the top was the Easy World logo, which says, "I live in Easy World, where everything is easy." Then I put "The ideal publisher for *Choosing Easy World* is magnetizing it *now,* with ease! Our job is just to stay in Easy World, act when inspired, and allow the magic to happen!" And at the bottom was "Breathe . . . relax . . . allow . . . enjoy." It really helped me *allow* instead of trying to force things. And since you're reading this book, you can see that it worked!

- **Make a habit of choosing Easy World when you're about to go to sleep at night, and when you first wake up in the morning.** Choosing EW right as you're dropping off to sleep ensures that you are in optimal allowing mode because while you're sleeping, the Difficult World Dictator is not able to interfere.

    Choosing EW first thing in the morning gives you your best

Breathe . . . Relax . . . Allow . . . Enjoy

possible start and helps you create a harmonious day. Putting a reminder on the ceiling above your bed for you to see when you first wake up can be very effective, and putting one on your bathroom mirror or on the wall you face when you're . . . um . . . "sitting on the throne" works great, too!

- **Set reminders on your mobile phone or computer to choose Easy World.** There are many free time-management applications available on the Internet.

- **Designate a mug as your Easy World reminder mug** and always use it to drink your morning cuppa—and your afternoon and evening beverages, too. As you drink, you might say something to yourself like "With each sip, I move deeper and deeper into Easy World, where everything is easy."

  You might want to use glass or ceramic paint to write the EW magic words on your mug, or you can find official Easy World mugs and other Easy World paraphernalia in the Easy World Boutique at www.ILiveInEasyWorld.com.

- **Find an Easy World partner** or partners and commit to reminding each other to choose Easy World. Having other people as a support system is very effective and powerful. I can't tell you how many times other people have successfully reminded me, the Easy World messenger, to get myself back to Easy World!

- **Download Easy World computer "wallpaper"** (background for your computer's desktop) and a screen saver so that whenever you look at your desktop, you'll be reminded. (Get these on the Freebies page at www.ILiveInEasyWorld.com.)

Breathe...Relax...Allow...Enjoy

- **Keep this book handy.** Having it out where you can see it will serve as a reminder, and when you feel you need an Easy World pep talk, reading a few pages will help bring you back to where you belong!

MANAGE YOUR INFLUENCES

The fastest way I know of to find yourself in the depths of Difficult World despite your best intentions to the contrary is through an invitation to your fearful ego from another fearful ego or egos. Start noticing where those invitations are coming from, and either minimize your exposure to those sources or plan in advance how you're going to stay in Easy World when you encounter them.

Once you've created an Easy World–dominant life, you'll find that due to the Law of Attraction, your invitations to Difficult World will have diminished. Your EW reality will attract more influences for staying in Easy World instead. It's pretty much impossible, however, at this point in your straddling of the worlds, to avoid invitations back to DW altogether. But you can inoculate yourself by simply recognizing the possibilities and making sure to choose Easy World as your default.

I have found that there are certain places where I seem to be more vulnerable to the DWD than others if I don't make a point of preparing myself first. After figuring this out, I've taken these measures: First, I go to those places only when I

Breathe...Relax...Allow...Enjoy

absolutely need to, and I make a point of not going at times I may be especially susceptible to the Difficult World energy.

Second, I remember to center myself and move into observer mode so that I'm not so liable to be sucked in at a visceral level. Third, and most important, I make sure to choose Easy World before I go (and as many times as needed thereafter), and I actively radiate Love unconditionally as I go about my business. What a difference! So just pay attention to your own Difficult World Waterloos, and make the necessary adjustments. Here are some likely sources of DW invitations:

- **News outlets.** The mouthpieces of Difficult World. The old cliché that the guiding credo of newspaper editors and TV news directors is "If it bleeds, it leads" is clear evidence of this. The Difficult World Dictator is utterly obsessed with drama, trauma, danger, and catastrophe—and potential catastrophe. They are the perfect invitations into his world.

    The more lurid the details, the more tantalized the reptilian-brain-driven ego is. Spend as little time as possible feeding your fearful ego in this way. Be aware that, at this point in history, consuming the news is simply increasing the influence of the DWD in your life, and guaranteeing that you are in Difficult World.

    So, consider not immersing yourself in the newspaper, TV, or online news sites. Your fearful ego will try to keep you addicted to the news by telling you that you might miss something important if you don't partake. That's just another ploy to keep you entrenched in Difficult World. If there is something you truly need to know, you can absolutely trust your Spirit to guide you to that knowledge in another way.

If it scares you, upsets you, makes you angry, or otherwise invites you to a lower vibration and out of Easy World, close the newspaper, turn off the TV, or click over to a different Web site that supports your being in Easy World!

- **The political arena.** Involvement in politics is something you may want to limit as it is an area that is truly seductive to the DWD. Because it's all about who's right and who's wrong, the DWD is not only right at home in politics, he also feeds heartily on it.

  The duality-driven concepts of right and wrong are purely ego-based, and when you get caught up in them, you are definitely in Difficult World! If you immerse yourself in politics, be wide awake and aware that when you judge others as right or wrong (and yourself as right!), you are in the clutches of the DWD.

  If you find the political arena irresistible, as I myself often have, particularly during U.S. presidential elections, be sure that you maintain the posture of an observer, keeping in mind that while you believe you can clearly see what "ought" to happen, only when you are at the highest vibration can you really see the whole picture. You can't be at that highest vibration or in Easy World when you're judging and in resistance, and politics is all about that!

Breathe...Relax...Allow...Enjoy

- **Your entertainment sources (movies, TV, games, books, music, etc.).** Notice whether they are inviting you into Easy World or Difficult World. Since DW is so prevalent in the mass consciousness, and since the very reptilian quality of greed currently dictates so much of what goes on in the entertainment industry, entertainment that is designed to appeal to the masses is usually geared toward the DWD. *And,* it is influenced in its creation by the DWDs of others!

But there are entertainment sources that are less so, and certainly an increasing number that are uplifting—that support us in raising our vibrational level. Choose that which invites the feeling of Love, as it is transcending the DWD's resistance to allow Love to flow more freely within you. If it engenders fear, anger, or sadness, you can know that it is feeding the DWD and contributing to keeping you mired in Difficult World.

I'm not silly enough to think you're going to give up your favorite entertainment cold turkey if it is based in Difficult World concepts, but just be aware and make your choices consciously instead of by default.

As you spend more and more time in Easy World, your choices of entertainment will naturally evolve to match your new preference for being at a higher vibrational frequency. Meanwhile, maintain your role as an observer and don't get caught up in anything that works at cross-purposes with your intention to live an Easy World life.

Breathe...Relax...Allow...Enjoy

- **The people with whom you spend your time.** Choose them with an awareness of whether or not you feel uplifted in their presence (and vice versa). Some associations tend to call forth your fearful ego, and others bring out the more enlightened you.

  While it's true that choosing Easy World more and more will naturally attract people that are a vibrational match for your high-vibe self, and repel those who are not, in the meantime, you will want to be sure you're not handicapping yourself unnecessarily.

  I'm not suggesting you chuck your old friends and associates overboard, but when choosing whom you're going to spend time with, you can enhance your chances of staying at a higher vibrational frequency by not hanging out with those whom you notice bring out the DWD in you.

  Sometimes we continue to associate with people out of habit, loyalty, or a fear of letting go. Be assured that the Universe will fill any vacuum created by releasing what doesn't match the new you with people who will.

  While we can't replace our families if our response to being with them is to be in Difficult World, we can minimize the time we spend with them if need be, and modify our own responses to them so that when we're with them, we don't allow ourselves to get sucked into a de-evolutionary vortex!

- **Driving, especially in heavy traffic.** This seems to bring out the DWD in even the most centered, loving, kind, polite individuals! The freeway is something of a playground for people's egos, and

Breathe . . . Relax . . . Allow . . . Enjoy

there are almost always invitations to come "play." The anonymity of being on the road, enclosed in a vehicle, seems to embolden the reptilian-brain-driven ego so that people act out in ways they never would in more personalized situations.

Obviously, you can't avoid driving, but you can do what you can to choose times that are less hectic on the road. You can be aware that you are likely to be provided with some invitations from the DWD, and you can choose Easy World right from the start, and keep choosing Easy World. (This is where having a reminder note in your car will help.)

Instead of reacting passionately when someone else does something your own ego doesn't like, you can maintain your role as an observer and refuse to get caught up in it. You can simply *decide* to take a chill pill! One of my favorite ways to rise above my irritable ego in such situations is to feel compassion for the struggles of those caught up in Difficult World—because I live in Easy World, where everything is easy!

- **Alcohol, and places that serve alcohol as the main attraction.** Such spots are particularly attractive to the DWD, and are rife with opportunities to suck you into Difficult World.

A little bit of alcohol can anesthetize your ego and get it to drop resistance so that your outgoing, friendly self moves to the fore. But a little bit *more* alcohol can drop your vibration and bring out your least enlightened aspects and induce them to cause—or join in with—trouble.

And then there are the other folks who are drinking who have not yet made being in Easy World their intention! Whether

Breathe...Relax...Allow...Enjoy

it's just bickering with a friend, getting involved in a barroom brawl, or all kinds of stuff in between, disharmony occurs because the DWD is empowered in these settings. So be aware of this dynamic and make your choices accordingly.

CREATE A SUPPORTIVE ENVIRONMENT

The atmosphere that surrounds you is more important than you may think in staying in Easy World. While your environment is a reflection of where you are in consciousness, your environment can change your consciousness as well. It can uplift you.

If you've ever rearranged a room, you know what I mean—it gives you a different feeling, and a new perspective. And if you've ever cleaned up and organized a space that really needed it, you know how it frees up your energy and gives you that clichéd "new lease on life." It's simply *empowering*.

When I was in the process of seeking an agent and a publisher for this book, I shoveled out, cleaned, and reorganized my office in preparation for the job ahead. It definitely supported being at a higher vibrational level, and shifted my whole outlook. My office had been pretty grubby, and not having all the clutter, dust, and out-and-out obstacles to moving around the room freed up my psyche and made it far easier to be in Easy World! I even magnetized a large, like-new desk with matching bookcases, and all they cost was the rental for the truck to go pick them up.

Breathe...Relax...Allow...Enjoy

You see, my old desk had been falling apart, and it was just too small. I knew it was time for a new desk, but we didn't have it in our budget for one. When the large, beautiful desk Rick's mom gave away when she downsized—the one I had kind of hoped would be mine, but had never really asked for—had gone to Rick's sister, I turned the matter over to Easy World and let go in confidence that I'd have a better desk soon. *Somehow*. Meanwhile, I knew that cleaning and sorting out all the stagnant piles clogging my office would free up some energy, so I plowed into them.

When I was about halfway through my cleaning-out process, Rick got an e-mail from his sister. She had decided to move to a place where there wouldn't be room for the large desk and bookcases she had recently received from their mom, and, without even knowing I had wanted the desk, she was offering them to us. They were ours for the taking! I'm writing this book atop that very desk.

My "new" clean, organized office with my new large desk really changed my outlook. It has made my environment more pleasant, efficient, and energized, and the Easy World delivery of the desk was yet another reinforcement for me to not only trust in Easy World magic, but also to want to share Easy World with you!

Whether in your home, your workplace, or your vehicle, that which surrounds you impacts your vibrational level and your ability to stay in Easy World. It impacts you psychologically, emotionally, and physically, as well as spiritually. Take a look

Breathe...Relax...Allow...Enjoy

around and see what in your environment may be working at cross-purposes with your intention to live a life of ease and joy, and do what is necessary to upgrade the situation. Let Easy World help!

- **Getting (and keeping) your environment clean and organized is tops on the list of ways to uplift yourself,** and it doesn't cost anything to do except a bit of time and energy. Dirt and clutter are indicative of stagnant energy, which blocks the healthy flow of energy.

  Whatever it takes, clear out all the stuff that isn't contributing to the peace and clarity you could be feeling if it weren't there. There are several helpful, motivating books on clutter clearing from a feng shui perspective, and I have used them myself to make a huge difference in my environment. (Feng shui is an ancient Chinese system of balancing and promoting optimal energy flow.)

  Once when Rick and I were trying to figure out how we could afford to buy a house, we shoveled out our storage room (which, according to feng shui, was in the prosperity sector of our apartment), got rid of lots of stuff that we'd been hanging on to for no real reason, and organized the rest. Within a week, a source of money we hadn't thought of presented itself, and we were house-hunting in earnest! Within a year of purchasing our house, the mortgage was paid off! *Easy World.*

- **Arranging your room so that it is balanced and feels harmonious creates a balanced, harmonious feeling within you.** And

Breathe...Relax...Allow...Enjoy

that's conducive to staying at a higher vibration and in Easy World. If this is an area in which you need help, invite a friend who is a natural at interior design to advise you, or, if you can afford it, hire an interior designer.

Once again, look to feng shui for guidance on arranging your space to create greater harmony, health, and prosperity through creating optimal energy flow in your spaces. You will find that looking at your spaces with an eye to enhancing energy flow and creating visual balance will automatically ensure that they are comfortable, attractive, and conducive to your being in Easy World.

- **Light, bright spaces support being joyful.** Letting in as much natural light as possible to start with, and supplementing with other lighting, gives you your best chance of having happy, healthy days.

  Use full-spectrum lightbulbs in your light fixtures. They provide the complete spectrum of wavelengths of the sun's light, which will help keep the hormones that affect mood in balance, and they are just better for you all around. Full-spectrum light stimulates your pineal gland, which is your connection for experiencing higher realms—that is, Easy World!

- **Color greatly affects your energy and mood.** Make sure that the colors you're living in feel harmonious and uplifting to you. One of the most impactful and economical things you can do to create an Easy World–supportive environment is to paint your walls in a color that you love and that makes you happy.

  Choose livelier shades for spaces that are meant for being

Breathe...Relax...Allow...Enjoy

alert and active; more subdued, peaceful shades for those spaces meant for rest. Full-spectrum paints are the paint version of full-spectrum bulbs. They mimic Nature by including the seven colors found in natural sunlight in every shade. This creates a balancing and uplifting effect.

Before you paint the walls, try using the paint to write words like "Love," "joy," "peace," and, of course, "Easy World" on them, and then paint over them. You won't see the words once the walls are painted, but their energy will be there and you'll know they're there as blessings for the room.

If for some reason you can't paint your space, you can use colorful draperies, wall hangings, paintings, and other accessories to help shift the energy. You may also want to do some research into color therapy and using colored lights to balance and heal.

- **Diffusing therapeutic-quality essential oils can help you stay in Easy World** by moving your energy forward to the frontal lobes of your brain (and keeping it there), thus shifting your mood and stimulating your pineal gland.

  You can choose oils whose fragrances energize you, oils whose fragrances calm you, and oils whose fragrances help you feel more spiritually attuned. (See the "Aromatherapy" section of the Frequency-Raising Support Tools and Techniques in Chapter 7 for more on essential oils.)

- **Infusing your space with uplifting music** (as I also discussed more thoroughly as part of the Frequency-Raising Support Tools and Techniques) can keep you buzzing along in Easy World.

Breathe...Relax...Allow...Enjoy

Employ Holistic Self-Care Strategies for Health at Every Level

Living in Difficult World has certainly taken its toll by creating stress on our systems, and this has resulted in diminished over-all health for everyone. Whether you have major health challenges or are just not as hale and hardy as you could be, know that you are not alone. Everyone has been affected by DW's influence to some degree.

Easy World will automatically reduce stress and contribute to the restoration of health, but you can help that along. The healthier you are in all aspects—body, mind, and emotions—the more conducive to being in Easy World. Being as comfortable as possible in your skin is definitely empowering.

Basically, any of the modalities designed to enhance the health and well-being of your body, mind, and emotions will have the effect of raising your vibrational frequency and supporting your Easy World life. With the burgeoning of holistic and alternative approaches to almost every aspect of life, there is a lot to choose from.

I'm not even going to attempt to cover them all, but I'm sure you already know of many and will be guided to any others that will be beneficial for you. I'm just going to hit the highlights of some things for you to consider. You can absolutely trust your Spirit to nudge you in the direction of those that will be most helpful and effective for you.

Breathe...Relax...Allow...Enjoy

- **Drinking an optimal amount of pure water,** free of chlorine and other chemicals, is important not only from a mechanical standpoint, but also from a vibrational one. Water is a grand conductor of electricity, and you are designed to be a radiant, electromagnetic entity. Being hydrated is a requirement for being at higher vibrational frequency.

  Optimal hydration is necessary for a multitude of other reasons as well. You just can't be healthy and comfortable in your skin if you are dehydrated! Do some research into drinking water to determine what type will work best for you.

- **Fuel your body with high-quality, whole, natural foods** that work for you. Some foods help you move higher vibrationally, and some depress your vibration.

  Diet is a highly individual thing, and what causes one person to thrive can lead to illness or nutritional deficiencies in another, so finding your own best eating plan is a matter of attuning yourself to your own body and experimenting. To find the foods that are just right for you, you will have to take into consideration a range of factors such as likes and dislikes, tolerances, allergies, climate, emotional issues, body type, and more.

  You probably already know some of your dietary guidelines—not from reading some rule book, but from paying attention to your own responses to various foods—so build on those to discover how to eat in such a way that you feel your best. Ask your Spirit to guide you to your optimal foods and way of eating for supporting your being in Easy World.

  You'll want to look into increasing the amount of organically

Breathe...Relax...Allow...Enjoy

grown, raw, living foods you consume, since they require the least energy to digest and assimilate and promote reaching a higher overall vibrational frequency. Instead of robbing you of Life Force the way devitalized foods do, they add to it. Indeed, when I experienced cosmic consciousness spontaneously in Switzerland, I'd been eating a raw vegetarian diet for weeks. People who eat a high percentage of raw, plant-based foods are some of the most high-vibe, radiant, easygoing folks on the planet!

Also, using a high-quality sea salt, with its full complement of minerals intact and in balance, instead of plain sodium chloride (as is commonly found in the grocery store), which has been stripped of all other minerals, will support your operating at a higher vibration.

And one more dietary suggestion: Consider minimizing your refined sugar and carb intake. Not much invites the DWD in as effectively as a blood-sugar crash after an indulgence in the white stuff!

- **Eliminating toxins,** and the physical and mental stresses they cause, will assist you in reaching and holding a higher vibrational level. Keeping your elimination regular is vitally important, as is internal cleansing.

A constipated, toxic body is no help at all to being in Easy World—this is something I know from personal experience! A lack of trace minerals is often the culprit here, so be sure you're getting your quota. If a healthful, high-fiber, whole-foods, mineral-rich diet with plenty of water doesn't do the trick to

Breathe...Relax...Allow...Enjoy

keep you regular, there are helpful supplements to be found at your natural-foods store.

Something else to consider is that our bodies are exposed to a plethora of highly harmful toxins daily. These come from a variety of sources, including the environment, the food we eat, the medications we take, and unnatural substances we come in contact with every day, such as petroleum-based products—even the fillings in our mouths.

Over a lifetime, our bodies accumulate a health-defeating, vibrational-depressing toxic load that simply needs to be cleaned out. There are myriad internal cleansing techniques that address different bodily systems and different toxin types; be sure to consult your health-care provider for guidance.

- **Use natural, organically produced body-care products**. Essentially, if you wouldn't eat it, don't put it on your body. Your skin absorbs what you put on it, so if you wouldn't eat a petroleum product, don't smear products that contain petroleum products such as mineral oil and petroleum jelly or any other toxic ingredients on your skin.

How does this impact your intention to be in Easy World? In a couple of ways. One is that you'll stay healthier if the products you use—in all areas of your life—are natural and toxin-free. Also, participating in commerce with companies who are creating their products out of a higher awareness and with your health in mind makes you part of a higher vibrational reality and puts you closer to Easy World.

Breathe...Relax...Allow...Enjoy

- **Hormonal balance is important to health** at every level of your being. When your hormones become *imbalanced,* your health, including your energy level and your mood, is impacted. This makes it far more challenging to get to Easy World.

  This is much too complex a topic to even begin to cover thoroughly, but I'd like to encourage you to look into this if you're experiencing challenges like low energy, radical mood swings, PMS, or menopausal or other symptoms that may point to a hormonal imbalance.

  These can be addressed with nutritional support and other natural approaches. I have personally found help from using all-natural, bio-identical hormones prescribed by my doctor (after a panel of tests to measure my hormone production). You might want to do some research into these. They can help both women and men with hormonal balance at any stage of adult life.

- **Get enough sleep.** Sleep is the gift we are given daily to return to Easy World without interference from the Difficult World Dictator. It is how we routinely get our fearful ego-minds out of the way so we can realign with Source, and so Life Force can freely flow through us. This is one of the main reasons why sleep is so healing and rejuvenating—it's when we drop resistance and come fully back into the Design for Harmony, align with the divine patterning for our health/wholeness, and receive a full measure of Love/Life Force to enliven us.

  When we sleep, we are in Easy World as long as we truly let go and relax. Getting enough sleep is extremely important in raising your frequency and keeping it high so that you can easily

Breathe...Relax...Allow...Enjoy

access Easy World during your waking hours as well. Never underestimate the power of a full night's sleep or a nap when you find yourself in DW!

- **Be sure you're not letting fear keep you in a situation that doesn't serve you.** If you're in any kind of partnership, including marriage, or in *any* situation that doesn't support your being in Easy World, ask yourself why. The continual drag on your vibration caused by a mismatched relationship or other stressful situation is a boon to the fearful ego.

  This goes for jobs, too. If your work situation is not supporting you in expressing your personal genius, if you're not valued and/or respected there, or if it is, in any way, making it a special challenge to be in Easy World, you need to either change your own approach or consider that it's not the right match and trust your Spirit to guide you to a situation that will suit you better. Don't let fear of change—or fear of any kind—keep you from Easy World!

- **Treat yourself with the utmost respect.** Honor your own energy, honor your own Spirit's guidance over all other input, trust yourself, and put your own needs first. I know this is contrary to what is taught in our society, but guess who is behind that so-called selfless, put-yourself-last teaching? Yep. The Difficult World Dictator. He knows that if you put others first and yourself last, you'll end up depleted, frustrated, and resentful, and then he's got you right where he wants you.

  Just like the flight attendant says while delivering the safety instructions before the plane takes off, get your own oxygen mask

Breathe...Relax...Allow...Enjoy

working before trying to help someone else. This is not at all advocating being thoughtless and inconsiderate; it's simply being sure you first attune yourself with your own Spirit, move into alignment with the Design for Harmony, and meet your own needs. That way, you'll feel genuinely magnanimous and ready, willing, and able to share your Love and your bounty with others.

An important part of honoring and respecting yourself is speaking to yourself with kindness and compassion. Support yourself by not fussing at yourself or using any kind of abusive language with or about yourself. Speak only lovingly to yourself. You are, after all, a beloved and vital citizen of Easy World, and you simply can't be there if you're treating yourself poorly! Besides, only the DWD is abusive.

There are also these key components to staying in Easy World, which were featured in more detail in the Step-by-Step Frequency-Raising System:

- **Keeping your emotions in balance** by letting your feelings flow is crucial to being in Easy World. Express your emotions as they arise instead of stuffing them down.
- **Exercising on a regular basis** keeps your energy moving freely, oxygenates your brain, releases endorphins, and generally supports your wholeness and vibrational level in myriad ways.
- **Relaxation** is one of the major requirements for being in Easy World, so making it a priority is vital.

Breathe...Relax...Allow...Enjoy

- **Radiating Love unconditionally** on a regular basis will keep you in Easy World and transform your life in ways that you probably cannot fathom!

TRUST THE PROCESS

There are many, many more ways you can support your Easy World life. I'm sure you're already doing some of them, and you can bet your Spirit will be steering you toward others. I love the adventure of discovering strategies that help me stay in Easy World, and I know you will, too!

The payoff to this exploration is nothing less than a whole new level of living. Once you've sufficiently assimilated an Easy World mind-set, have adopted habits that support an Easy World life, and have reached a higher vibrational set point because of it, you will ultimately be able to stay in Easy World and dip into DW only when you decide to. Nice, huh?

I choose to live in Easy World,

where everything is easy.

Breathe...Relax...Allow...Enjoy

10

Easy World Q&A

ven though I've done my best to give you a thorough overview of Easy World, I know there is no way I could have covered everything you might wonder about it. While living an Easy World life will enable you to grasp its nuances and directly receive the answers to any questions you might have about Easy World, perhaps my sharing some of the questions others have asked, along with my answers to them, will be helpful in the meantime!

Is Easy World a physical place?
Yes—and no. Easy World is whatever physical place you're in when you choose it. It exists simultaneously with Difficult World, and shares physical space with it. Just like your TV set plays host to both Channel 1 and Channel 2 (and a multitude of

Breathe...Relax...Allow...Enjoy

other channels) but only fills the screen with one channel at a time, so your physical world is host to multiple realities. Though Easy World is *vibrationally* and *perceptually* separate from Difficult World, it is wherever you are when you decide to be there.

The chaos and disorder that seem to characterize where you are when you're in Difficult World will shift as you choose Easy World. Because being in Easy World upgrades your perceptions to be a vibrational match to the Design for Harmony, it changes how you perceive what you look at. Easy World is a far more beautiful and harmonious reality, so you will see that beauty and harmony reflected in your surroundings—the same surroundings that were not so beautiful and harmonious when you viewed them in Difficult World. Don't be surprised if when you're in Easy World, things seem more vivid and lustrous and even smell better!

My couch potato cousin's almost forty. He got fired from his job a year ago and isn't looking for another one. He lives with his mother—who does everything for him—and he mooches off everyone and never lifts a finger! Does he live in Easy World?

For this answer, you'll have to ask your cousin! My guess is that if he's being honest, his answer would be "No." It sounds to me as if your cousin is stymied by life, which is a painful condition not experienced in Easy World.

While it's true that he has somehow found a way not to have

to do anything but is being supported anyway—which could be described as an Easy World scenario—the *true* measure of being in Easy World is not inactivity, but experiencing joy and fulfillment doing that which you're inspired and energized to do. I would guess this is not the case with your cousin. There are few human beings who would be truly fulfilled for very long in the situation you're describing.

There is certainly a tendency among human beings to feel resentment for having to work for a living because we still have a primal connection to the time when everything was provided for us simply by virtue of our beingness—the time before we began our adventure in Difficult World. Your cousin may be feeling this. But I don't think he's experiencing Easy World.

Having everything provided for us without effort is still a viable option for us when we choose Easy World, but it never comes at anyone else's expense—including our own soul's. Ultimately, our fulfillment is unlikely to come when we're stuck on a couch in front of the TV!

If I don't push at my job, I won't get ahead or get a raise— don't you have to work hard to be productive?
Our work/reward system was designed in Difficult World—to *keep* us in Difficult World—and we've collectively wandered so far from Easy World that we hardly know anymore what true productivity is about. But just notice that the most productive, most successful people use an economy of motion, and work "smart," not "hard." They stay attuned to their inner genius,

Breathe...Relax...Allow...Enjoy

and while they may not claim to be following the guidance of their Spirits, they are, nonetheless.

As for earnings, the wealthiest people are seldom the ones who work the *hardest*—instead, they are the ones who most enjoy what they do and apply themselves passionately and tenaciously to doing it. They may put in many hours, and while they may interpret that as "working hard," it is more a matter of immersion and time, with any perception of difficulty likely coming more from the lack of balance they've developed in their lives than their actual money-making activities. It is entirely possible to maintain your balance, do what you are passionate about, and make lots of money—in Easy World.

The Difficult World Dictator is going to lie to you and tell you that pushing and working hard and doing things you aren't cut out for is the way to get ahead. The truth is that doing what you love doing—doing what supports your joy—and staying aligned with the Design for Harmony and in the rhythm of the flow of Love brings true success and fulfillment. If you aren't doing something for work that fits that description, consider that you may have followed the dictates of the fearful ego to where you are now. Being less than joyful is the state the DWD wants you in.

Consider surrendering the whole thing to Easy World and letting your wise Self steer you to your rightful place in the Design for Harmony, step-by-step and in a way that helps you maintain your equilibrium. Doing so means that you'll be guided to do that which will be most fulfilling not only to you, but also

Breathe...Relax...Allow...Enjoy

to the Whole, and when you are supplying the needs of the Whole, you will always be richly rewarded *as long as you allow yourself to be.*

Couldn't I just rob a bank and live in Easy World?

No. Robbing a bank is definitely not Easy World–sanctioned!

Because Easy World is based on the Design for Harmony, and the Design for Harmony is about supporting the well-being of everyone and everything, stepping outside of integrity is not supported in Easy World. You are automatically evicted from Easy World if you are dishonest, inconsiderate, disrespectful, or threatening, or in any way lacking in integrity. Being in alignment with the Design for Harmony keeps you in Easy World.

If you robbed a bank or committed another crime in the past, you can certainly choose to be in Easy World *now* as long as you have cleared out the issues within yourself that caused you to step outside of the Design for Harmony in such a dramatic way. But you have to be willing to live in integrity and align yourself with the Design for Harmony in order for Easy World to be available to you. You can't reach the vibrational level of Easy World if you're not.

Can I get my husband (friend, sibling, coworker) to join me in Easy World if he doesn't believe in it?

Sure. But you don't get to dictate anyone else's perceptions of Easy World. If you're on Channel 1 and he's there, it means he's

Breathe...Relax...Allow...Enjoy

there, whether he's consciously aware of it or not. He doesn't have to choose Easy World in order to be in your EW "cast of characters." If he's in your scenario while you're in Easy World, it means he's in Easy World, too.

After all, there's an aspect of him—his Spirit—that's always in Easy World, just like there's an aspect of you that always is. Whether you're perceiving *that* Self or his ego-influenced self is a matter of your own vibrational level and vantage point. So, if you notice that he is not plugged in to the Design for Harmony—if he's being anything less than an agent of Easy World—it means that *you yourself* have left Easy World! If what you're seeing is Channel 2 (Difficult World) behavior from someone else, it means you're tuned in to Channel 2 and need to choose Easy World again.

It's great fun, of course, when your loved ones consciously embrace Easy World and you can choose it together and feel the companionship of other people who are willing to let go and be in Easy World. But the key to having company in Easy World really has nothing to do with that and everything to do with being there yourself. Then, everyone you meet will be in Easy World, too. If they're not, you know *you're* the one who needs to get back to Easy World.

And one more thing to be aware of: Sharing your knowledge of Easy World can be a very helpful, appropriate thing to do, but it's important not to let sharing become pushing. Only tell people about Easy World when you're inspired to, and know that they'll catch on if and when it's time for them to. If you buy

Breathe...Relax...Allow...Enjoy

them this book, don't bug them to read it—trust their own Spirit to nudge them to read it when the time is right for them!

If the economy is in crisis, is it possible to be in Easy World?
Not only is it possible, it's the place to be! There is no crisis in Easy World, economic or otherwise—ever. Crisis is a construct of the fearful ego. The DWD thrives on crisis and will always seize on every chance he gets to put you in crisis mode. That provides rich food for the fearful ego. The more invested in a particular Difficult World idea you are, and the more you're buying into the DWD's PR about it ("Times are tough"; "There aren't enough jobs to go around"; "The stock market is tanking"; "We're running out of money"; "These are desperate times"), the more real it is going to seem.

These notions may be true in Difficult World, but they're *absolutely* not true in Easy World. As I've reminded you many times, DW rules do not apply to EW. Whatever is going on in Difficult World has nothing to do with the constant perfect provision of Easy World. There is always exactly enough of everything in Easy World. There's never lack of any kind there. None whatsoever.

Conditions in Easy World are always supportive of your well-being. Always. So don't be alarmed when the DWD starts applying scare tactics. Just use it as your cue to move into Easy World so you can receive the bounteous blessings and everyday magic to be found there!

Breathe...Relax...Allow...Enjoy

I'm involved in a legal matter. Does EW work with that?

Easy World works for everything. In general, the legal world isn't particularly conducive to being in Easy World because it is based on duality principles that aren't supported in Easy World. But that doesn't mean that harmonious, easy solutions to legal situations can't be found in Easy World—they can. It just means that you will need to rise above the ego's tendencies to be angry, afraid, and judgmental in order to truly be in Easy World. But that's always the case!

Of course, if the legal matter you're involved in came about because you did something while you were acting without integrity, and your goal is to avoid taking responsibility, you won't find that supported in Easy World. Easy World is about integrity (wholeness) and harmony, so things that are inconsistent with those states of being are inconsistent with being in Easy World. If, however, your goal is to achieve a fair solution that supports the well-being of all involved, choosing Easy World is definitely the way to go in legal matters and matters of every kind.

Isn't it just lazy to lie around and wait for inspiration?

The concept of laziness doesn't exist in Easy World. It is uniquely Difficult World. In fact, it's a trap. It's just another one of ego's devices to keep you out of the realm of ease. As long as you are in Easy World, attuned to your Spirit's guidance, willing to take action when inspired and energized, any *in*action on your part is exactly what is being called for according to the Design for Harmony.

"Lying around, waiting for inspiration" hardly characterizes the typical Easy World scenario, anyway. If lying around is what you truly want to do and it brings you pleasure, then great! Absolutely lie around. If you're doing it out of rebellion or for any other reason than that it's what you really want and feel guided to do, then you're not in Easy World. Resisting action (or inaction) is not being in Easy World.

The more typical Easy World scenario is that you're pursuing activities that interest you—that you love doing—or that simply feel right in the moment, and when inspiration strikes to do something else, you obey that and act on it.

There are times when I'm involved in a project that I'm really excited about and I can feel I'm in Easy World, but suddenly, I feel resistance to doing something I know I want to do. What's that about?

That's just an indicator that it's not yet time to do that part of the project and you need to move to a part of it that you feel like doing—that you feel no resistance to doing. If you feel resistance to doing *anything* on the project, but you still feel committed to it, it's time to walk away for a while and do something that appeals to you, something that is joy-promoting, and know that you'll be attracted to the project again when it's time.

Remember that in Easy World, only inspired, energized action is in alignment with the Design for Harmony. Remind

Breathe...Relax...Allow...Enjoy

yourself that your idea of when to do something may not line up with the actual optimal time to do it—the time that will coordinate with the Design for Harmony. When you trust your energy and interest to indicate when to do something and when not to do something, you coordinate with the Design.

There are often things I have to do that I don't want to do, but if I don't do them, nobody will. How does that fit into Easy World?

First of all, I would advise you to suspend your disbelief and limited thinking! Your belief "If I don't do them, nobody will" is *creating* that experience for you—it's creating it in Difficult World. That's one of the reasons knowing about Easy World is so powerful. You can have the belief "If I don't do them, nobody will" in Difficult World, but at the same time, know that it's just not the way it is in Easy World. Always remember that *DW rules do not apply in EW.*

Easy World has all kinds of resources—infinite resources—that you can't wrap your mind completely around. Sometimes the marshaling of those resources on your behalf will seem downright miraculous; other times, less so. Sometimes the thing you thought you didn't want to do simply evaporates and no longer needs doing. When you've chosen Easy World, someone else may unexpectedly appear to do something you don't want to do.

Sometimes, the thing you wanted to avoid doing becomes something you enjoy doing if you simply change your approach

Breathe...Relax...Allow...Enjoy

to it. When you resist something, it will indeed seem difficult, unpleasant, and not at all enjoyable. When you drop resistance and move into Easy World with something, it can become a joy.

Whatever the case, anytime you are doing something you don't want to do, it's a matter of being out of alignment with the Design for Harmony. When you align with the Design, everything shifts so that you do only that which fits for you, and that which does not is done by someone for whom it does.

Someone I love recently died. How can I possibly be in EW?
I know this may, at first, sound harsh, but if you aren't in Easy World for *any* reason, including the loss of a loved one, it's because you've chosen, albeit unconsciously, to be in Difficult World. This choice, of course, is based on the input of your fearful ego and the fearful egos of others. When a loved one passes on, it's pretty much assumed, in modern society, that if you're not already there, you will immediately move into Difficult World.

When someone close to you dies, it provides the fearful ego with a lot of rationales for digging in. The fearful ego absolutely has a thing about abandonment, and when someone important to you goes away, he or she trips the abandonment trigger. Abandonment equals certain annihilation to the aspect of you that is fed its lines by the survival-driven reptilian brain.

Then there are the messages about lack. The DWD will tell you that because this person is gone, you will never have the love you felt with him or her again. While it's true that your

Breathe...Relax...Allow...Enjoy

relationship with that person was unique, the love you experienced with him or her was actually not—unless you don't *allow* yourself to feel it again. Love comes only from Source—not from another person. The only reason you're not feeling that Love is because your fearful ego is using the loss as yet another reason to resist the flow of Love. It is vital that you allow Love to flow again because that's how you move out of DW and into EW.

A very spiritually focused friend of mine's husband died suddenly of a massive heart attack in her presence. While his death was a shock, her experience of it was transcendent and Love-filled. This carried her through the ensuing days, helping her deal with all the plans and logistics such a situation requires with relative ease. She was feeling his support and presence through it all, and experiencing all kinds of magical occurrences.

But when those around her kept telling her she should feel sad, and implying that she was dishonoring her husband by not being more upset, she finally succumbed to the DWD. When she did, she lost the amazing feeling she'd had of her husband's presence and closeness, and all kind of things became difficult—until she moved back out of Difficult World and into the clear light of Easy World again.

I think it's important to recognize that you are not dishonoring loved ones who have passed on if you opt out of Difficult World and choose Easy World. In fact, you are honoring them. After all, they've released their ego along with their body and

Breathe...Relax...Allow...Enjoy

are no longer in Difficult World! You will be far more able to experience a close connection with your loved ones who have passed on if you transcend your own ego and choose Easy World. And here's some food for thought: What if you could be having the experience of closeness you are missing, but you're hanging out in Difficult World instead?

Please do not mistake that I told you the story about my friend's experience to say that you should not be sad or that you should forgo the grieving process. I just want you to know that not only is it possible to approach the passing of a loved one without immediately sinking into Difficult World, but also that you can allow yourself to move to a higher vibrational level—to be in Easy World—even in the midst of such a transition if you choose to.

It is for sure that at some point, your fearful ego will need to express itself. Sadness at transition is a normal part of what it means to be a human being with an ego. But hanging on to sadness instead of processing it will only keep you in Difficult World indefinitely. I can promise you that your loved one would not appreciate that!

Easy World or Difficult World—it's *always* your choice, even when you're convinced it's not.

I have a terminal illness. How can I possibly be in Easy World?

When you become acutely aware that life as you know it is drawing to a close, it is going to stir up your fearful ego. Remember

Breathe...Relax...Allow...Enjoy

that its chief influence is your reptilian brain, the part of you that is all about physical survival. Impending death is tops on its list of reasons to sound the alarm and go into resistance. As always, however, it's a *choice* whether to be in DW or EW.

Many people in your situation report that facing this most dramatic of all transitions allows them to drop their ego resistance and embrace their Spirit as never before. When you fully realize that neither your logical mind nor your fearful ego can save you, you may well be motivated to turn to your transcendent Self and surrender to its guidance. In addition to our physical survival mechanism, we humans do have the instinct to seek our higher power when we are desperate!

The pronouncement that an illness is terminal is based on a limited view of what is possible—a limited view based in Difficult World; one that excludes the problem-solving, miracle-producing power of Easy World. When you go ahead and surrender to your Spirit and choose Easy World, you move into the Design for Harmony and are subject to its healing, harmonizing forces. Whether or not this leads to *physical* healing and life extension, the joy of this—of being in close alignment with your Spirit, flowing along in the moment and trusting the process—is surely preferable to the pain of resistance and fear.

Even if moving from this physical reality into a new one is the next healing step for you, already being in Easy World to do it means your experience of your transition will be far easier. Instead of being excruciating the way it is when one stays in resistance, it can be ecstatic.

Breathe...Relax...Allow...Enjoy

I have children—how can I stay in Easy World and not worry?
There is a special facet of the survival-oriented, reptilian brain's program that specializes in ensuring that you are protective of your children, and supplies extra juice for that. This is part of the human design. But this same facet activates your fearful ego around this and fuels the very Difficult World activity of worrying. And worrying is worrying, regardless of the object of your concern.

To worry is to put your faith in exactly what you *don't* want to have happen. Worrying is channeling your Life Force and creative power into fueling a hologram that the fearful ego is encouraging in order to keep you stuck in Difficult World. What you give your focus to increases in your experience. It increases proportionally with the amount of energy you're giving it. When you worry, you are making up scenarios that you don't want to have happen, and empowering them through thinking about them and adding your passion to them.

Worry is a lose-lose proposition. You can protect your children far better by moving into Easy World, where your well-being and the well-being of your children is always supported at the highest level.

Don't bad things ever happen in Easy World?
No, they don't. Only harmonious things happen in Easy World.

I must take exception with the term "bad" however. "Bad" is a judgment term that only your ego uses. For that matter, so is "good." Sometimes things happen at our ordinary level of ego-

Breathe...Relax...Allow...Enjoy

influenced awareness that we don't immediately like or don't understand. These, we characterize as "bad." When you're in Easy World, however, you are able to see the harmony and perfection in all that occurs. In Easy World, you won't be describing things in terms of bad and good—if you are, it means you're not in Easy World.

All that occurs in Easy World is harmonious and is what we might judge as "good" *if* we were to judge things in Easy World.

Whatever judgment terms your ego wants to use, only that which is in alignment with the Design for Harmony can occur in Easy World. Be assured that most of the time, you will like these occurrences, both when you are in Easy World and when you are out of it.

What if I'm not worthy of Easy World?
That's impossible. "Worthiness" has nothing at all to do with Easy World. Your *ideas* about your worthiness or unworthiness may keep you out of Easy World, but there is no gatekeeper other than yourself that is pronouncing you as either. The notions of "worthy" and "unworthy," and their companion concepts of "deserve" and "don't deserve," are created and sustained by the fearful ego to keep you at lower vibrational frequency. They are judgments, and only ego judges.

The DWD uses the worthiness/unworthiness myth as just another device to keep you in Difficult World, his domain. For the sake of reassurance, I will tell you that no matter what you have done or haven't done, or who you are or aren't, you are

Breathe...Relax...Allow...Enjoy

eligible to receive all the Creator's blessings simply by virtue of your existence.

No one—and I mean *no one*, no matter what he or she has done—is excluded from Easy World except by his or her own ego. Easy World is an equal opportunity reality. When you transcend the accusatory, judgmental voice of the DWD and get to Easy World, you will understand this. When you're in Easy World, it is crystal clear.

Isn't Easy World just a fun idea you made up?

No. I am not nearly smart enough—at least not at the level of my ordinary human consciousness—to have made up something so huge, dynamic, and amazing. Easy World existed long before I was made aware of it, and will exist always. While the name Easy World is not only perfectly descriptive but also cute, a little sassy, and tailored to be attractive to the human consciousness, I didn't come up with that, either. It was provided to me in the event I told you about in Chapter 1. I can't tell you with any assurance who planted the name in my mind, but whoever it was—an angel? my Spirit?—certainly is a marketing genius!

One of the (infinite) cool aspects of Easy World is that it doesn't matter if you think it's just a nifty concept but doubt that it's a real phenomenon. Choosing Easy World will work for you anyway—Easy World is always working for everyone, all the time. It's just a matter of whether you'll be relaxed and open-minded enough to tune in to it. You can certainly create plenty

Breathe...Relax...Allow...Enjoy

of evidence that it is *not* real—after all, you and your fearful ego have been masterfully creating the illusion of Difficult World for most of your life. And it's for sure that your ego will gladly cooperate with continuing to perpetuate your immersion in DW.

But I'd like to challenge you to at least temporarily drop any doubt or cynicism you might be experiencing about Easy World—that's the Difficult World Dictator at work, trying to keep control of you—and prove that it *is* real. You've got absolutely nothing to lose, and a life of greater ease, joy, and all manner of desirable things to gain!

I choose to live in Easy World,

where everything is easy.

Breathe...Relax...Allow...Enjoy

11

Adventures in Easy World

*A*ccounts of some of my personal Easy World adventures are woven throughout this book, but I'm not the only one with EW stories. Everyone I know who has discovered Easy World has tales to tell of its magic. Since I first rediscovered Easy World in 2007, lots of people have found their Easy World connection.

Just after I had my first official Easy World experience—the one I told you of in Chapter 1 when I received the divine whisper that reawakened me to the power of Easy World—I blogged about it and also shared it with people in a popular online forum. To my surprise and delight, folks took to it like ducks to water, and word of Easy World began to spread rapidly!

I started an online Easy World forum so that we could support one another in living Easy World lives and share our Easy

Breathe...Relax...Allow...Enjoy

World stories, and so there would be a place for people to come and learn about Easy World. It proved to be quite the powerful magnet, and we soon had hundreds of participants. Not long after starting the forum, I realized that Easy World needed a Web site of its own, so I created one (www.ILiveInEasyWorld.com).

The launch of the site was a hit. I had so much traffic that I wondered how it was possible. I had sent out an announcement to my list, but I had many more visitors than the mailing statistics would indicate. Then I heard from several people that they had been so excited about Easy World, they had forwarded my announcement to everyone on their own lists! Easy World at work.

To this day, we have a continuous stream of visitors to the Easy World site from all over the globe, with very little, if any, energy expended to get them there—except, perhaps, by Easy World itself! Easy World certainly seems to want to make itself known, not just to a select few, but to everyone.

It isn't just the spiritually inclined who are into Easy World. Even those with no metaphysical orientation, no consciousness of creating their own reality, and no awareness of the possibility of parallel realities have been experiencing "aha!" moments upon hearing the term "Easy World."

It stands to reason that Easy World is universally recognized and accepted—after all, it's humanity's original home. As someone put it on the Easy World forum, *"Everyone* gets Easy World—if they were dogs, their ears would prick up when they heard the words!"

Breathe...Relax...Allow...Enjoy

Indeed, beyond the Easy World following that has built up from the Web site, the forum, and the teaching I do, Easy World resonates with the people I encounter on an everyday basis. One telemarketer who called ended up asking me about Easy World and pumping me with questions about it instead of telling me about what she was selling! She then thanked me profusely for telling her about it, exclaiming that her calling me must have been destiny!

Whenever I wear my Easy World T-shirt out to do errands, people stop me to ask about it. They light up when I give them my quick explanation of Easy World: "Life wasn't meant to be hard—we've *made* it that way. But we can choose to live in Easy World, where everything is easy, instead!"

FIELD REPORTS FROM EASY WORLD

Immediately upon its inception, the Easy World forum started attracting an abundance of reports of people's Easy World experiences. It was so gratifying for me—and so inspiring for all of us—to read how choosing Easy World was working in the lives of others. The accounts, which were about all facets of life, helped us stay in Easy World, and comprehend the scope of its limitless possibilities to transform our lives.

A recovering alcoholic reported that Easy World was helping her stay sober. A cancer patient in remission said Easy World helped her stop worrying about a recurrence. The daughter of a "very negative mother" said choosing Easy World had changed

Breathe...Relax...Allow...Enjoy

their relationship. A teacher said being in Easy World had made grading papers, something she had always hated, a pleasure. A man who had been trying to lose weight said being in Easy World had helped him shed forty pounds.

A woman posted that when her furnace's pilot light went out on a cold winter day and she couldn't relight it, she invoked Easy World, and before she could even call anyone, a friend happened to stop by and was able to fix it. A secretary said her boss had lost his luggage, and she'd been frantically trying to locate it when she remembered to choose Easy World. Shortly thereafter, he called to say she could stop looking—he'd found it. Another forum regular was amazed to find her car's dead-battery problem solved when she chose Easy World. Her partner, who she said was not normally one to take care of such things, had been inspired to have her battery replaced for her while she was at work. She was as thrilled about the change in her partner as she was about not having to deal with the battery!

Choosing Easy World profoundly changed one single mother's life, according to her excited first post. She'd gone from having no job, being completely stressed out about how to pay the bills, and considering taking a job that she knew she'd hate just to make money, to having her dream job just fall into her lap. Her new employer was in the very industry she'd long been wanting to break into, their offices were located only blocks from her home, and the job offered flexible hours and paid even more than she had expected!

A young man wrote that he and his soon-to-be bride had

Breathe...Relax...Allow...Enjoy

wanted to buy a house, but didn't have the money for a down payment. They had found the home of their dreams in the newspaper, and were a bit discouraged about not being able to buy it, but decided to go see it anyway. Since they were also going to be looking for a house to rent, he decided to invoke Easy World before they set out. They were thrilled and amazed to find out the owner of their dream home was willing to make a rent-to-own deal with them! They moved in shortly thereafter.

Two of the most common themes people posted about were no longer having to wait in line or deal with traffic problems when they chose Easy World. But one Easy World forum regular, who'd had to wait in line at a restaurant, had just prayed for some companionship, and while waiting had struck up a conversation with a nice stranger. They'd had an enjoyable lunch together, sharing inspirational stories, and parted ways as new pals.

Several of our Easy World friends reported that they were getting their families to join them in Easy World. One woman said that when her husband was having problem after problem with fixing his truck, she'd invited him to Easy World, but he'd declined, insisting that what he was dealing with just wasn't easy. She then released the whole thing. The next morning, he told her he'd fixed everything with ease. When she asked him why he'd suddenly been successful, he declared, "Because I'm in Easy World!"

A gentleman told us that his wife had called him in the midst of a total meltdown while shopping at a big discount

Breathe...Relax...Allow...Enjoy

department store. She was sobbing her heart out and he didn't know what to do. Then it dawned on him to tell her about Easy World, and he got her to say the invocation and take the EW actions. He said she snapped right out of it, calmed down, and went on to have a fruitful shopping trip, returning home in high spirits. Delighted, he added, "She isn't normally into the kind of self-help stuff I am, but Easy World really clicked for her!"

It was especially exciting to hear how children were taking to Easy World. A young mom said that her kids had made up an Easy World game, and had become experts at catching themselves—and their parents—out of Easy World and re-minding them to get back to it. (I can only imagine how thrilled their parents' DWDs must have been!) One poster's children had made up an Easy World song that they loved to sing, and now the whole family sings it. In fact, several people sent me Easy World songs they had composed!

Reading these confirmations of the effectiveness and univer-sal appeal of Easy World on the forum* each day was definitely uplifting. The energy was contagious, and it was such a thrill to see how rapidly Easy World was catching on. I especially loved that almost all posters either prefaced or concluded their sto-ries with "I love Easy World!" It became clear to me that the Easy World meme was not just a flash in the pan, or something

---

*The original Easy World forum is no longer in existence, but you can find a link to the current EW forum at www.ILiveInEasyWorld.com.

Breathe...Relax...Allow...Enjoy

that would be limited to a few, but something that was destined to grow.

MORE EASY WORLD ADVENTURES

Naturally, being a writer and a spiritual teacher, I began to think of writing a book about Easy World. As requests started coming in from people who wanted to read such a book, I decided to make it a priority. Even before I began mapping it out, I knew I wanted to include stories of others' EW adventures as well as my own, so I asked for submissions. When I started receiving them, I was thrilled to see what a variety of experiences they cover and how clearly they convey everyday Easy World magic.

You'll notice that most of these stories were written about incidents that had recently occurred. I believe it's a testament to living an Easy World life that when I asked for stories, the contributors did not have to rack their brains or reach back very far to come up with one! Many of these folks told me they had multiple Easy World stories to choose from and that it had been a challenge to pick just one to share. Such is the nature of choosing Easy World. The magic is continuous!

AND NOW, THE STORIES . . .

You might want to share this first one with your child. Indeed, we might all take a lesson from young Mack; he is truly an EW citizen,

Breathe...Relax...Allow...Enjoy

as is his super-cool mom. When faced with having to choose among the many items on his list of his desires, he refused to settle for less than having it all. And he was able to get it all—in Easy World!

HAVING IT ALL IN EASY WORLD

From Marcy Koltun-Crilley ("Marcy from Maui") (www .MarcyFromMaui.com)

My son Mack's birthday was coming up and he wanted several pricey things. On his list was a Freebord (a type of skateboard), a new skimmer (a board you do tricks on at surf's edge), and a big beach party. He was also hoping to have another Waveski (a sit-upon surf rider) in the family so he could join me when I took mine out.

All those things would normally total well over $2,000, and other than the party, were not readily available on Maui, where we live. (The type of skimmer he wanted is not sold here, nor is the Freebord or the Waveski.) So we told him we would give him the party and $200 to spend on whatever else he wanted.

He couldn't make up his mind because he passionately wanted *everything*, but we agreed to just relax, let things flow, and stay in Easy World.

The next day, Mack got a call from a friend who is sponsored by the skimmer company. They said they would give him a skimmer at half price, include the shipping, and allow him to trade it in as he grows in return for sponsorship. (He was very excited about that because being sponsored by water-sports companies was another thing on his list of desires!) The price for the skimmer came to $200!

We had the party, and he got $275 in cash as gifts.

We then found a Freebord online and it cost $250 with shipping, so he ordered it.

Right after that, he found a new Freebord on Craigslist, which was the style he really wanted, with all the upgrades, and for only $175, but he had already ordered the other one. He was starting to feel bad because he would have liked to have had the local one plus the extra money instead, but we talked about it and, once again, agreed to just relax, let things flow, and let Easy World handle it.

The next day, we got a call from the Freebord store. They had not yet sent the board due to a shipping issue. So we were able to cancel the order. Since the other board was local, we got it that night. In fact, we picked it up just a few minutes from our house!

Finally, that same day, I found a Waveski on Craigslist. The woman who was selling it was only asking $90 for it. She lived a few minutes from us as well! When we went to see it, it was just what we wanted and would not only fit my son perfectly, but would also expand for him as he grew!

So within a week, my son got all he asked for perfectly, in Easy World, of course!

This next story, provided by an adventurous young Polish man living temporarily in the United States, illustrates the power of choos-

ing Easy World and moving forward in complete trust that all will be handled, even when it is not obvious how. It also shows the power of simply appreciating Easy World. I think you'll agree that things could hardly have worked out much better for him as a result!

THE ODDS ARE ALWAYS IN YOUR FAVOR IN EASY WORLD

From Maciek Wronski (maciek.wronski@yahoo.com)

Last Friday, I went to Philadelphia to extend my visa. My friend gave me a ride there, but he couldn't drive me back home. And the office I went to is . . . well . . . I don't even really know where it is! So I started to worry about how to get back to my place. First of all, I live an hour away from Philly, and second, I don't know Philly at all!

But then I said, "I live in Easy World, where everything is easy." I repeated this phrase a few times on our way to Philadelphia, not because I was still worried, but because saying it makes me feel so good!

When I got to the visa office, I asked them about the best way for me to get home. They told me *there would be a bus going from right in front of their office to my neighborhood!* I was like "Oh my God, that's just impossible!!!" What are the chances?

But then they said it was leaving in *three and a half hours.* What was I going to do to fill up all that time? So I said to myself, "Okay, it's not a problem. I'm quite sure this is going to be

Breathe...Relax...Allow...Enjoy

a very nice three and a half hours." And you can guess what happened—it was the nicest three and a half hours *ever*!

First I had an interesting conversation with guys from that office. Then I went for a walk and found a Polish church. There was nobody inside but me, so it was really quiet. I enjoyed studying the beautiful stained glass windows telling stories about saints who had lived in Poland. Time was going so fast. It was really cool.

And do you know what? This is not the end of the story. When I bought my ticket for that bus, they told me it was going to a casino in Atlantic City, where I live, and that the casino was going to refund the money for the ticket! Can you believe it? I paid $17 for the ticket, and the casino gave me back $20!

This is just amazing! I LOVE Easy World and I'm so grateful I can live in it!

We don't like to think of things such as what happened in this next story as happening in Easy World—or in Difficult World, either—but who knows why things happen the way they do? Patricia chose Easy World and affirmed its miracle power, and she got to experience an EW miracle!

As you'll see, for someone going through something so potentially traumatic, her experience was about as easy as one can imagine. It serves as a wonderful reminder to always choose Easy World before driving.

Breathe...Relax...Allow...Enjoy

EASY WORLD SAVES LIVES

From Patricia Russell (www.PMRussell.com)

Since I've begun following the basic principles of living an Easy World life, things have become easier—even things that, at first, don't look like they'll be easy at all. Last weekend, my husband and I were traveling at night, at around eleven P.M., from Saint Louis to our home in southern Indiana. As a small blessing, before we got in the car, I said to myself, "I live in Easy World, where everything is easy and where miracles happen."

It was a beautiful fall evening. We were in good spirits and knew to watch for deer since they were quite active at that time of year. We were traveling in a group of cars in a rural area on a major interstate. We were making a point to keep our speed down and to be cautious. We had just left a nice awards banquet for my company and were heading home to our ten-year-old son.

We were halfway home when it happened. One minute, we were driving along in peace, and the next minute there was a loud bang. The air bags deployed, and the car drifted off the highway and stopped. It all happened in a matter of seconds. The last thing I saw before the air bags deployed was the face of a deer.

When the car came to a stop, my husband asked me what had happened. He had seen nothing since the deer had come from the passenger side, outside of headlight range. It had apparently jumped onto the hood of the car. My husband said that he had no idea how the car got so easily to the side of the road. We got out of the car to assess the damage. What we saw shocked us.

The vehicle was totaled. The front end was completely demolished. It was a mass of twisted metal. The hood had somehow come up and blocked the deer from entering the cab, where we were sitting. The windshield had caved in right up to our faces without touching us. The driver behind us pulled over because he had seen a deer leg fly past him. The impact was so great, the deer had exploded.

The good Samaritan who stopped called 911 for us and drove us to a nearby hotel, where we waited comfortably for a relative to pick us up. The police officer who wrote up the accident report said he could hardly believe we had walked away from the accident unharmed. He said that he'd seen many deer-related accidents and this was one of the worst. In most cases like this, the deer goes through the windshield, killing the occupants. He had never seen a hood fly up like that.

We weren't even inconvenienced by the loss of our car. We had been driving a rental car, and the insurance filing went without a hitch. Later, at home, I researched deer-related accidents. Just that week there had been numerous fatalities. Most happened when the deer went through the windshield. In all the pictures I checked, not one had a hood that had opened up to block the windshield.

Not only did we come out of the accident unharmed, we are

living proof that miracles *do* happen. Living in Easy World makes *everything* easier!

This next story of Easy World magic inspires me to hope that all *parents will learn to do their parenting in Easy World instead of letting the DWD raise their precious children! Note the way this single mom from Australia dealt with her little boy's injury at school. She's an Easy World natural.*

HOW AN EASY WORLD MOM
HANDLES A TRAUMA

From Sandy Lee Jones (www.lovecreateinspire.com)

In my life as a mother, I have found that choosing Easy World is an absolute necessity.

Earlier this year, I was on my way to pick up my son, Michael, from preschool. I was in high spirits—definitely in Easy World—and I got on a different bus than usual, one that would get me there a little earlier. Just before I arrived, I received a call to alert me that Michael had fallen off the jungle gym and was injured. They wanted me to come to the school right away. I was very glad I'd gotten the nudge to take the earlier bus and was already almost there.

Instead of getting upset, I stayed in Easy World. I relaxed and trusted completely that everything was in place to support us to travel through this experience with ease.

Breathe...Relax...Allow...Enjoy

I arrived to find my son in extreme pain, crying uncontrollably like I'd never seen him do before. He managed to say a few words about his arm, and I let him know he was going to be fine. The teacher kindly took us to the local doctor, where Michael was met with kindness, stickers for his arm, and a bravery award. He took the medication they gave him, whereas normally he wouldn't have.

We had the added challenge of then needing to travel to a hospital about half an hour away, without a car, to get an X-ray of his arm. We managed to get a taxi right in front of the doctor's office, with a kind lady driver who reassured Michael that he would be okay.

When we arrived, we were taken to the children's section of the hospital. We had many hours ahead of us, but the Easy World angels had seen to it that there was a video of Michael's favorite children's show to watch. As soon as he saw it, he laughed and was himself again, his focus off the pain. He even cracked some jokes! (I discovered that day that laughter provides an access to Easy World.)

We went in for the X-rays, and Michael was incredibly patient as they took photos from different angles. The X-rays indicated that his arm was fractured. The doctor was in positive spirits and said that it would probably heal naturally. He advised against surgery at Michael's young age.

Michael's arm was covered in a cast, with a sling around his neck. He was a little unhappy about this since he couldn't move his neck, but soon he settled down and understood it was helping his arm. After the very long day, I bought him a milk shake, his favorite treat. It was long after bedtime and we were both pretty worn out at that point.

I was unsure if I had enough money for the taxi ride home, but I just trusted that I did. We arrived home after midnight, exhausted but still in Easy World. Amazingly, and without knowing how much money was in my purse, the driver was guided to give me a few dollars off the fare, which turned out to be the exact amount I had left!

I am very sure that my choosing to be in Easy World, and my certainty that everything would work out, brought calmness to my son and helped us both get through the experience with a minimum of stress. When we have fear, anxiety, or concern or label something as "bad," we miss the doorway to Easy World.

My experience has taught me that to respond with Love instead of fear when we encounter any situation, and to trust that we are always being taken care of, assures us of a life that truly fulfills us and brings us joy every day.

The next story is pure Easy World fun! But it's not just fluff— Suze's level of stress at trying to please was no laughing matter. Take a cue from this story and let go of trying to make *exciting things happen. In Easy World, all you have to do is relax and allow* them to.

Breathe...Relax...Allow...Enjoy

A CELEBRITY SIGHTING IN
EASY WORLD

From Suze Baez (www.SuzeBaez.com)

Not too long after I learned about Easy World, a couple of my girlfriends—Tobi from Las Vegas and Wendy from Oregon—came for a surprise visit. I live in California, not far from Los Angeles, in an apartment overlooking the beach, so I am no stranger to playing hostess. I was excited for them to come so we could just hang out and play and have some "girl time." My boyfriend was happy to bow out of the picture to give us space to do our thing.

I was ready for a nice, relaxed, play-it-by-ear visit, but Wendy arrived with a bit of an agenda. She was absolutely intent on seeing a celebrity! Now, I'm forty-five years old and have lived in Southern California all my life, and I've never encountered a celebrity just out and about. I didn't exactly know how to go about arranging to spot one; I mean, it's not like there's some reference you can turn to that tells you where to spot celebrities at any given time!

But Wendy was totally obsessed with the idea. So I got on the phone and started placing calls. I called friends of mine who are celebrity stylists, but no luck. I called everyone I knew who might have a line on an opportunity to see a celeb, but no luck. I even tried to get tickets to *The Tonight Show with Jay*

Leno—no luck. My boyfriend knew I was stressing out, but he said, "You're on your own with this!"

Wendy, however, would not be deterred. She was absolutely convinced that her visit would not be complete without seeing a celebrity, and she brought it up constantly. At this point, I was tearing my hair out. My vision of a relaxed girls' weekend had been shattered. I had spent most of the first day of their three-day visit on the phone, and I was stressed to the max, trying to make things happen to please her. I so very much wanted them to have a fabulous, unforgettable time. Finally, when it was clear to me that this frantic approach was simply not working, I surrendered.

When I went to bed that first night, I said to myself, "This is just ridiculous! I live in Easy World, where everything is easy, and Easy World will just have to handle this." The next morning, I printed out more Easy World reminder posters from ILiveInEasyWorld.com and put them up in every room to remind me to chill out. I kept the Easy World invocation going like a mantra!

Then I realized that instead of focusing on pleasing Wendy, I needed to just plan the rest of the visit to be the kind of relaxed, easy time *I* would love to have. So I did.

That day, we went into L.A. to my favorite Thai massage place, and we each had a fabulous hour-long massage, for only fifty dollars each. When we emerged, we were so relaxed, we were like limp noodles. We were all three in a state of bliss—so much so that Wendy proclaimed, "Even if I don't see a celebrity, I'll be okay."

Breathe...Relax...Allow...Enjoy

Next, we went to the famous Bodhi Tree bookstore on Melrose in West Hollywood (which is not exactly the upscale part of town) and enjoyed poking around their huge selection of metaphysical books. After that, we decided we needed food, so we got a table on the patio at the café next door. Suddenly, we heard what sounded like a mob of people screaming and yelling in the distance. As the sounds got closer, we could clearly hear a chorus of "Paris! *Over here,* Paris!" and "You look *stunning,* Paris!"

It was the paparazzi—dozens of them—swarming everyone's favorite celebutante, Paris Hilton. In all my life in this part of California, I had never encountered the paparazzi before!

Paris and her entourage passed right by us—within inches—and went into the café. They stayed for about half an hour before leaving (with the paparazzi still following, of course). She was posing and preening and milking it for all it was worth. As her car pulled away from the curb, about twenty cars were tailing hers. It was the ultimate Hollywood celebrity sighting, and all we'd had to do to experience it was to be in Easy World!

I'm sure I don't have to tell you that Wendy was beyond thrilled. We all were! It was so perfect and so funny and such a great demonstration of the power of letting Easy World arrange things. We laughed and laughed and couldn't stop saying, "*That* was easy!" like the voice on the Staples Easy Button.

As the icing on the cake, minutes later I got a call from my boyfriend, who said he'd arranged for us to fly up the coast in a helicopter the next day to a friend's ranch to shoot skeet. On the way back, we spotted a pod of about fifty dolphins, and the

Breathe...Relax...Allow...Enjoy

helicopter pilot circled around so we could watch them. It was magical. The visit did turn out to be unforgettable!

It is just mind-blowing what happens when you relax and allow Easy World to deliver!

Michelle's story illustrates that an Easy World experience doesn't have to be big or dazzling in order to provide major insights, or to prove the power of choosing Easy World!

THE WAY IS ALWAYS CLEAR IN EASY WORLD

From Michelle Smith

One recent morning, my daughter and I both overslept, which meant she missed the bus and I had to drive her to her high school. Both of us were grumpy and snappish since neither of us is a morning person. We hit every red light on the way.

Once I'd dropped her off, it took what seemed like forever for anyone to give me a break to get out of the parking lot onto the main road. Once there, wouldn't you know I was instantly boxed in by slow, lumbering, exhaust-belching school buses? Grrrr!

As we inched toward the traffic light, I felt myself getting even more resentful and out of alignment.

In a flash of inspiration, I stopped myself and (mentally) blurted out the first random positive thought I could get hold of: "Wait! I live in Easy World, where everything flows smoothly!"

Breathe...Relax...Allow...Enjoy

Right then, the two buses in front of me (the one directly in front of me and the one beside it) put on their turn signals and turned off the main road—one to the right, one to the left—and suddenly the road in front of me was clear!

Wow. What an awesome, impossible-to-miss message!

I think you'll find Jacqueline's story of dealing with a life-altering situation—one that is pretty much guaranteed to stir up the fearful ego in any of us—to be downright heroic. Notice that even though fear was constantly nipping at her heels, especially when things seemed to be going very wrong, she just kept choosing Easy World.

OUR HOME IN EASY WORLD

From Jacqueline Stone (www.Squidoo.com/JacquelineStone)

After a chain of unexpected events, including the exit of my husband, my house went into foreclosure. I did everything I could to work it out with the lender, to no avail. The house foreclosed and was immediately sold at auction. I was in utter shock and disbelief as the process server told me we had to be out by Thanksgiving, with only six days' notice. My two children and I had nowhere to go. Suddenly, Difficult World, and all its fears, had me by the throat.

Fortunately, I had already learned about Easy World and frequency-raising techniques. It took all the spiritual strength I could muster to apply them and move out of fear. I took lots

Breathe...Relax...Allow...Enjoy

of deep breaths and repeatedly turned everything over to Spirit. I deepened my daily practice of expressing gratitude, looking for every possible thing to be grateful for.

I also focused my attention and energy on being Love and radiating Love, and I must have declared my choice to live in Easy World a thousand times a day! I constantly reminded myself of how Spirit is always providing for me and guiding me to the right next step. As much as I wanted to stay in our house, I let go of resistance, and let whatever happened be okay.

Through a series of unusual synchronicities, I discovered there was a class action suit against the lender who had foreclosed, and I ended up going to court, where the judge ordered a trial to contest the validity of the sale of the house. That meant that no matter what happened, we could stay in our home at least until after the trial, a month later. We would be there through the holidays. A relief!

Just before the trial, I found out that my application for legal aid couldn't be processed till after my trial date. Miraculously, the judge quickly changed the date to a month later, giving us even more time before we might have to move. Meanwhile, I put a deposit down on an apartment. I really didn't feel it was the right place, but at least we'd have a place to go if we were ordered to vacate.

The next step in the process was a trial management meeting, in which the judge told me that based on the evidence, I would not win the trial. For a multitude of reasons, I knew that pursuing the matter further was not the right path for me. Bottom line:

Breathe...Relax...Allow...Enjoy

We were losing our house and we'd have to leave it. Normally, I would have gotten only a week to move, but the judge asked the attorney to extend it to three weeks. Instead, the attorney extended it to a month! Some more breathing room.

My response to the news that we'd definitely have to leave our home? To my surprise, I felt liberated and empowered! It seemed right to be leaving the vestiges of the old life behind. I was even strongly guided to go and tell the apartment manager that we wouldn't be moving in, and I got my deposit back. Though we had nowhere else to go, I knew that the apartment was just not right.

Despite the evidence that some would say indicated things were going wrong, I felt a strange confidence that things were lining up for us even though I couldn't yet see where we would be going.

As the weeks passed, I kept choosing Easy World, but I'd be lying if I told you I was always there! I kept checking the newspaper for rentals, and nothing was right. What was I going to do? I had my children to think of.

Still, something inside me kept telling me that all was well and just to trust. With only a week left to move, and still no place to go, I was getting more concerned with each passing day, finding it increasingly difficult to get to Easy World.

Finally, on the verge of being totally exhausted from trying to resist the fear, I gave it *completely* over to Spirit. I just dropped the burden and said, "I trust you to handle this."

Less than an hour later, out of the blue, I received a phone call from a man who goes to our church who had heard of our plight

Breathe . . . Relax . . . Allow . . . Enjoy

and said he and his wife wanted to rent their house to us at a price we could afford! They had bought a new house and needed someone they could trust to live in their old one. Amazing.

Suddenly, we had a home to go to that was as nice as the one we were leaving, my kids could stay in their same schools, and on top of that, we were providing a service for these kind people. An Easy World win-win! And all those time extensions from dealing with the court? If we'd had to find a place any sooner, the house we were offered to rent would not yet have been available!

What a blessing to have a fresh new start in Easy World! Now not only are my family's needs being met, but the needs of others I didn't even know about are being met, too. Living in Easy World is not just for our own peace, joy, and harmony. It really does touch the lives of everyone around us. Our choice to live in Easy World, and to trust Spirit no matter what the appearances are, changes *everything*.

Now it's your turn. I'm sure you'll soon have lots of Easy World stories to share. I know I'll be excited to read them!

I choose to live in Easy World,

where everything is easy.

Breathe...Relax...Allow...Enjoy

12

An Easy World Planet

You now know that if you have decided to embrace Easy World, your life is about to be transformed into one of more Love, more joy, more ease, more peace, more fulfillment, and more prosperity. Exactly *how* that will impact your own experience and the course you take in your life truly boggles the mind to imagine! The possibilities for experiencing blessings in all aspects of your life just by choosing and being in Easy World are infinite.

A thrilling thing to contemplate, too, is that not only is your *own* life about to be transformed by choosing Easy World, but the possibilities for transforming far *more* than just your personal experience are also endless. Imagine how the lives of everyone in your circle—your friends, your family, your coworkers, and all those you cross paths with—will be impacted because

Breathe...Relax...Allow...Enjoy

you have decided to choose Easy World and relax and align with the Design for Harmony.

Simply being more at ease, more patient, more efficient, more authentically confident, and less controlling, the way you are when you're in Easy World, will make a huge difference in your interactions with others. This, in turn, will have an effect on the interactions *they* have going forward, and so on. Just seeing an Easy World–inspired smile on your face instead of a Difficult World–induced grimace, or hearing the kinder, gentler words you say instead of the words the DWD would like to channel through you may be the turning point in someone's day.

What if your choosing of Easy World and your interaction with someone from that place means they are able to be more relaxed and centered, too? What if their tender, impressionable child is greeted by a more easygoing, patient parent instead of a frustrated, angry one, simply because you set the tone by being in Easy World? I'm sure you can imagine the impact that might have.

What if the Love you're radiating by being in Easy World invites someone else to be more loving, too? What if your peacefulness influences someone to be more at peace within himself so that he doesn't give in to road rage or some other seduction from the Difficult World Dictator? What if your silent invitation into Easy World enables someone to find a solution to a problem she might not otherwise have been able to? What if the spiritual wisdom you experience in Easy World empowers you to help someone see his own truth? And on and on.

Breathe...Relax...Allow...Enjoy

The power of the ripple effect ensures that there's no end to the influence you have.

This is true when you are in Difficult World, too—then, your influence reinforces the dominion of the Difficult World Dictator. I'm saying this not to lay a guilt trip on you, just to make you aware of your power! *And* to reinforce the importance of choosing Easy World. When you're in Easy World, the possibilities for assisting *others* to experience more ease and joy simply by *your* being in Easy World are endless.

Now, what if by seeing the wonderful changes you undergo as you open yourself up to an Easy World life, and by witnessing the miraculous results of your making the choice to allow Easy World to handle matters with ease, even *one* person is inspired to also create an Easy World life? Imagine the influence that might have on everyone *she* interacts with, and, in turn, on everyone those people interact with, and so on! It's utterly impossible to know how far the ripples will extend.

Next, envision a planet where just 1 percent of Earth's approximately 7 billion people have decided to choose Easy World and live an Easy World life. On top of the practical ways we've considered that Easy World will spread, we need to factor in the exponential increase in the magnetic power of Easy World as it is amplified by more and more human beings. This attractive power draws people into Easy World even without direct contact with anyone who is already operating in the realm of ease. This makes your own capacity to transform the planet by choosing Easy World completely, utterly, unfathomably immense. And *easy*!

So, what kind of difference will it make when that many folks are consciously aligned with the Design for Harmony? What will happen when that many of Earth's citizens are deliberately relaxing and allowing? What kind of energy will that free up? How much will that uplift the whole of humanity? What kind of impact will the ripples caused by *that* have?

Why, the joy quotient on Planet Earth will surely skyrocket, along with all the other things we dream of for humanity—peace, prosperity, everything! Prosperity is a natural effect of choosing Easy World, since EW is where all one needs and desires is provided with ease. With ease always comes joy, and with ease and joy comes peace.

We all talk about world peace and think it's a good idea, but there's just no chance of having that until enough people are choosing Easy World and experiencing the joy that comes with living there. The DWD has absolutely no interest in peace since that robs him of some of his chief tools for keeping us in DW. Turmoil and friction are important factors in his domination!

In truth, Easy World is the only reality in which either joy or peace exists. Peace is not a feature of Difficult World. Period. Joy is not a feature of Difficult World, either, and joy is a prerequisite for peace. Have you ever heard about someone who did something violent or destructive because he had an easy, harmonious life and was authentically joyful? Have you ever

Breathe...Relax...Allow...Enjoy

known someone to beat his spouse because he was experiencing a state of bliss? Or start a war because he was so happy and fulfilled?

As more and more of us choose Easy World, world peace becomes a reality—not because we get together and decide peace is a good idea and make rules about peace, but because we embody peace and naturally, effortlessly facilitate that for others! It's a beautiful system; when we return to Easy World, we automatically open the door for others to do the same.

The only thing you ever really have to do to contribute to the transformation of life on Planet Earth is to be in Easy World. By doing so, you perform the highest possible service to humanity—and to yourself—that you can. Anything else you're inspired to do, however grand, will be gravy.

But the most thrilling aspect of this may just be that when *you* choose Easy World, *your* world is *already* peaceful. Your world is already joy-filled. Your world is already prosperous. Your world is everything you've longed for the world to be. It's already happening. You just have to be there to experience it. And everything else falls into place.

It all starts with you, choosing Easy World.

I choose to live in Easy World,

where everything is easy.

Breathe...Relax...Allow...Enjoy

Acknowledgments

There are many Easy World angels to thank for getting this book into form and out to its readers, but first in line must be Easy World itself, along with my Spirit—my personal Easy World guide—who empowered me to write *Choosing Easy World* and easily and efficiently make all the magical connections that have made this book possible. Thank you, thank you, thank you!

I found my wonderful, supportive agent, Lisa Hagan, by invoking Easy World and then entering *literary agent, spirit* in the Google search window. She was the first one listed in the results, and that has certainly proven to be no mere coincidence. She's not only performed magic, finding me the right publisher within mere minutes of sending out a query for *Choosing Easy World,* but her embrace of Easy World has been positively

Breathe...Relax...Allow...Enjoy

inspirational. (Read: Sometimes she's had to remind *me* to get back to Easy World!) Thank you, Lisa!

Through Lisa, St. Martin's Press came on board and Easy World gained the stewardship of the indomitable Jennifer Enderlin, editor extraordinaire. (I'm glad I didn't know her elevated status in the publishing world right away or I may not have been able to do more than stammer when she called me prior to making an offer to publish the book!) Jennifer immediately caught the vision and went to bat for *Choosing Easy World* and has never wavered in her belief in it, even when a couple of folks didn't get it. She's the editor of my dreams and clearly exactly who Easy World selected for the role of this book's midwife. I can't even begin to thank you enough, Jen, for the belief, the support, the enthusiasm, the patience, the artistic freedom, and the guidance you've provided!

Thanks also to the many other professionals at St. Martin's Press who have helped bring the book into being and out to the world. Special appreciation goes to the marketing department's Matt Baldacci and Tara Cibelli, as well as publicist John Karle, for your enthusiastic embrace of *Choosing Easy World* and for going the extra mile to make sure word of it spreads far and wide. Thank you, Sara Goodman, for handling the nitty-gritty details. And Mimi Bark, not only is your cover design radiant, you have the patience of a saint.

This book was definitely catalyzed by the many citizens of Easy World who have shown up on my forums, blog, and Web

Breathe...Relax...Allow...Enjoy

sites to share their energy, their Easy World experiences and insights, and encourage me to keep spreading the word about Easy World. I appreciate all you "early adopters" (or, should I say, "early returnees") more than you know. Extra thanks and deep appreciation go to the contributors of the Easy World stories found in Chapter 11.

When my first book came out, I got busted by one of my longest-running buddies because I'd neglected to mention some of my dear, longtime friends by name. I'm not going to make that mistake again! So, thank you, Lily Keyes, Stephanie Gage, Steve Gage, Michelle Rich Goode, Donna Michael, and Catherine Jourdan for the decades of love, support, and keeping me humble!

Speaking of keeping me humble, no one can do that quite so effectively as one's family of origin. And neither can anyone love you in quite the same way. Thanks to Dad, Bob Rogers, who is still here straddling the worlds with us; to Mom, Becky Rogers, who is with us in Spirit; and to sisters Ann Salisbury and Linda Haines for doing your job so well! Thank you for your continued unconditional support; you are the bedrock I build upwards from.

My darling stepdaughters, Aubrie, Allison, Wendy-Anne, and Claire: You know I adore you. You keep me on my toes and practicing choosing Easy World whenever I start to worry about you! Thank you for your love and acceptance. And for once and for all, *I do so like green beans!*

Breathe...Relax...Allow...Enjoy

For demonstrating what it looks like to choose Easy World in the face of a major life trauma—the death of a spouse—thank you, Brenda Williams, dear longtime friend. For showing me an amazing example of what is possible when someone comprehends the power of choosing Easy World in the midst of particularly harsh invitations from the Difficult World dictator, I am deeply appreciative of my friend Jacqueline Stone. Jacqueline, you've been a stunning mirror for me and a true inspiration. Yes, *you*.

Thanks also go to Tony Roberts, my awesomely accommodating webmaster; my highly intuitive friend Andrena Keesee for her continual affirmation of my career and the success of this book; Ellen Kennon, for her continuing support and enthusiasm for my work (her amazing Full Spectrum Paints are the ones I talk about in Chapter 9); marketing guru, TV exec, and cousin-in-law Glenn Marrichi, for great advice; and Maurice White, co-founder of Earth Wind & Fire, for knowing decades ago that one could raise the vibration of the planet with the right music. Maurice, your genius has certainly contributed to the high-vibe nature of this book!

The one person to whom I owe the greatest debt of gratitude is my husband and partner in life and business, Rick Hamrick. If I tried to list the infinite kindnesses you extend to me every day and the myriad ways you support me so that I can be and do that which I am called to, I'd need a whole other book to do it. Our love and friendship provides the foundation for everything I do and am. You are truly an agent of Easy World and I

Breathe...Relax...Allow...Enjoy

thank Spirit for you, your love and your big heart, every day. I'm also hugely grateful for your enthusiasm for my writing, your willingness to copyedit and proofread however many times it takes, and for the great job you do of it!

I am blessed, indeed.

I choose to live in Easy World,

where everything is easy.

Breathe...Relax...Allow...Enjoy